BITTER sweet

BITTER sweet

Winnie Mack

SCHOLASTIC INC.

First published in Canada in 2016 by Scholastic Canada Ltd.

ISBN 978-1-338-24635-3

12 11 10 9 8 7 6 5 4 3 2 1   17 18 19 20 21 22

Printed in the U.S.A.   40

This edition first printing, November 2017

Cover photo by Anna Prior

*For Ella, one of the toughest kids I've ever met
and for my hero, Mike Smith*

Chapter
ONE

My favorite thing in the world (and this includes warm brownies, sleepovers with my best friend Emily and stacks of presents under the Christmas tree) is soccer.

I love running down the field, my cleats digging into the grass, my arms pumping as I dodge the defense. The closer I get to the other team's goal, the more excited I feel.

Because I might score.

And nothing feels better than scoring for my team, the Strikers.

So when I woke up that Saturday morning, knowing it was game day, all I could think about was getting out on the field.

I was the first one up and in the shower. As I rinsed the strawberry shampoo out of my hair, I thought about what Coach Donaldson had told us at our last practice.

She was going to pick a team captain.

Team captain!

For as long as I'd been playing, the Strikers had *never* had a captain. As soon as I'd heard the announcement, a happy buzz filled my whole body. And I was still buzzing. I was ready to do everything I could to earn a white C for the shoulder of my jersey. I would run faster, shoot harder and be the best teammate I could be to make that C mine.

Samantha Stevens, Captain.

I loved the sound of that almost as much as the sight of the ball slipping past a goaltender's fingers.

I got out of the shower, dried off, then hurried down the hallway to the bedroom I shared with my little sisters.

When I opened the door, I groaned.

I'd only been gone fifteen minutes, max, but the clean room I'd left behind looked like it had been hit by a tornado — a tornado that had hung around for a while, bouncing from wall to wall, messing up everything in its path.

And I mean everything.

The girls had been playing dress-up again, so all of the stuff from their toy trunk was either dumped on the floor or hanging from the furniture. There was a sparkly boa on my desk, a pink tutu hanging from my study lamp and glitter all over the place — like the tornado had been armed with a Bedazzler.

I heard giggling from inside the pink tent by the window.

"Hey, you guys," I said. "You need to clean this place up."

My little sisters crawled through the flap, still giggling.

Zoe was dressed in a bright turquoise vest, plaid shorts that were ten sizes too big for her five-year-old body, a tiara that was missing most of its "diamonds" and a pair of purple cowboy boots. Most of her dark hair had come out of her ponytail and was sticking up all over her head.

Kate was wearing the monkey costume she'd trick-or-treated in last year. The furry suit was so hot, her bangs were stuck to her forehead with sweat. On her feet were the red-sequined shoes I'd worn for my starring role as Dorothy when I was eight. She was only seven but her feet were already too big for them, so she hobbled instead of walked.

"Mom's going to freak out when she sees this," I told them.

"Sees what?" Kate asked, hands on her hips.

I stared at her, then made a point of looking over the whole room. "Really?"

"Oh," she said quietly. "*That*."

"And I need my uniform," I said. It wasn't at the end of my bed, where I'd carefully laid it out before my shower. "Where is it?"

"Uh," Zoe said, then stopped.

"It's game day," I reminded her.

"I know," she said with a huge smile. "We made pompoms."

The next thing I knew, both sisters were waving clumps of green and yellow tissue paper in my face.

"That's great, but I need my uniform. Now."

They threw themselves into the search. But that didn't mean they stuck with it.

"I'm going to wear this when I'm a mermaid," Zoe said, picking up a shell necklace.

She was totally obsessed with mermaids and had decided to be Ariel for Halloween. *Again*. It was too bad; with her missing front teeth and pointy canines, she would have been an excellent vampire.

"I'm going to wear a jersey and shorts when I'm a soccer player," I told her. "In an *hour*."

"Okay, okay," she mumbled, continuing the search.

Luckily, it only took a few minutes to find my uniform. It was buried under a pile of baby blankets the girls used as shawls, wedding veils or whatever else they didn't have in the dress-up trunk.

The Strikers were the visiting team that week, so I put my reversible jersey on showing "away" yellow instead of "home" green.

After the jersey, I put on my shorts, shin pads and socks. I stretched the yellow knee-highs up as far as I could, then folded the tops over the elastic rings Mom had made to hold them up.

I left my sisters to find clothes they could actually wear out of the house, and I headed downstairs.

When I got to the kitchen, Dad was making pancakes, Mom was making coffee and my stomach was making a racket. I was starving, as usual. I started to pile pancakes on my plate.

"Just one at a time, Samantha." Dad laughed and looked me over from head to toe. "I don't know where you put it all!"

I grinned and watched as he hung up his apron and kissed Mom goodbye. He had to work on Saturdays, which meant he missed my games, but he was always happy to listen to a play-by-play afterward.

"Either you're heading for a growth spurt or you've inherited your dad's metabolism," Mom said, shaking her head.

"A growth spurt would be nice," I said, loading my pancake with a ton of blueberries.

While I ate, Mom moved behind my chair to braid

my hair. She always wove it super-tight, so not even one strand would come loose at the game.

She finished just as I popped the last blueberry into my mouth.

"Can you please get the girls?" she asked. "And let your brother know we're leaving in," she checked her watch, "twenty minutes."

"Aiden is coming?" I asked, surprised.

He barely ever came to my games. He thought ten in the morning was too early to be anywhere but in bed. Ever since he'd turned fifteen he slept more than our tabby, Tony. (And cats nap for something like fourteen hours a day!)

I ran upstairs to pull my family together so they could cheer me on.

I bumped into Aiden in the hallway. He was wearing the dark blue hoodie that never made the laundry, and he had so much product in his hair it looked like he'd just showered. It was kind of gross. Even worse? He smelled like the green toilet-bowl cleaner Mom kept under the bathroom sink. I'm sure his aftershave (does a guy who doesn't shave need it?) was driving the girls crazy, but not in the way he wanted it to.

He was overdoing it, but I didn't say anything. He'd have just told me I didn't understand because I'm not in high school yet.

Like twelve wasn't old enough to know when a guy was trying *way* too hard.

Kate and Zoe came out of the bedroom carrying their wilted pompoms and giggling, as usual.

"Ready for breakfast?" I asked everyone.

Aiden nodded, leading the way downstairs.

"Will you score a goal for me?" Kate asked, grabbing a plate and a pancake before settling into her usual seat.

"Yup."

"And one for me?" Zoe begged, sitting next to her, already searching for the syrup.

"One each," I told them. "I promise."

After all, two goals would only help my chances at making team captain.

* * *

I love every single minute of soccer. I love practices, pre-game warm-ups and the game itself. I love the moment when it's all over and we chant, "Two, four, six, eight, who do we appreciate?" I love walking single file past the other team, high-fiving everyone while we all say, "good game, good game, good game." (The Strikers usually say it a lot louder when we win.)

So when our minivan pulled into the Eastview parking lot that morning, I was out the sliding door before my family had unbuckled their seat belts. I took off running toward the rest of my team, smiling at the sight of all that yellow in the middle of the bright green grass.

"Samantha!" Mom called after me. "Oranges!"

Oops.

It was our turn to bring snacks for halftime. I turned around and jogged back to the van to grab the plastic tub.

When I carried it over to Coach Donaldson, I was glad she could see me doing my part for the Strikers.

"Thank you, Samantha," she said with a smile. "Are you ready to take on the Ravens?"

"Definitely," I told her, hoping I sounded like good team-captain material.

"I'm glad to hear it. They're a tough team, so we'll have our work cut out for us. Go ahead and join the rest of the girls for warm-ups, and I'll be over in a minute."

I grabbed a ball from her mesh bag and dribbled toward my teammates.

Most people were stretching, but I saw Alyssa and my best friend Emily passing a ball back and forth. Nearby, Brianne and Kylie were practicing shots on our goalie, Mai.

I waved to Emily and joined Brianne and Kylie to take some shots of my own.

Before I took my first shot, I closed my eyes and took a deep breath of fresh fall air. I could hear my teammates calling to each other and the soft thuds of their cleats kicking balls. As I opened my eyes, I could feel a grin taking over my face.

Game day.

I tapped the ball into prime position, took a few steps back, then ran forward and kicked it.

The ball soared through the air, heading exactly where I wanted it to go: the top right corner.

I'd spent a lot of time in our backyard working on my shot. Aiden was never around to practice with me anymore, so I'd been aiming at chalk Xs on our fence. I was glad to see it was paying off.

We spent a few more minutes shooting before Coach Donaldson blew her whistle and got us started on five laps around our half of the field.

As we ran, I kept an eye on the Ravens. Their black-and-white uniforms made them look tough, but that didn't mean anything.

Anybody could *look* tough.

But it turned out the Ravens actually *were*.

The first half passed in a blur of black and white, yellow and green. By the time we broke for water and a snack, we were hot, sweaty and only ahead by one goal.

A goal scored by Kylie.

"Nice shot," I said, wishing like crazy it had been mine.

"Thanks," she said, grinning. "That's seventeen so

far this season." I watched as she ran over to Brianne for a high-five, her ponytail swishing.

"Seventeen goals," I repeated quietly.

"You're playing awesome, Sam," Emily said.

"I need to score, though." I bit into an orange slice, then wiped its juice from my chin with my sleeve. "That number six is really fast."

"But you're staying a step ahead of her," Emily said, smiling.

"Barely." It was true. My legs were more tired than usual, and I was still trying to catch my breath.

"Barely's enough."

I grinned back. "Thanks, Em."

* * *

During the second half, I scored my first goal, so I was halfway to keeping my promise of one each to Kate and Zoe. But the Ravens were giving us a run for the money. They'd scored two goals back to back!

Before I knew it, there was less than a minute left to play. We were tied and I had the ball, thanks to a beautiful pass from Emily.

"Go, Samantha!" I heard Zoe scream from the side-lines as I dribbled down the field.

I squeezed between two Ravens and saw the goalie raise her gloves in my direction.

She was ready for me.

I tapped the ball one more time with the toe of my cleat and took a deep breath (which was hard to do because I'd been running like crazy). I eyed the goal, lined up the shot and kicked the ball as hard as I could.

It sailed through the air, and I bit my lip as I watched it squeak just out of the jumping goalie's reach.

"Yes!" I shouted as the ref blew his whistle and ended the game.

The rest of the Strikers ran over and pulled me into a half-hug, half-huddle, slapping me on the back. And they didn't let go until they'd pulled Coach Donaldson in.

When we'd finished high-fiving the Ravens, Coach told us what a fantastic job we'd done on the field and that she'd see us at the next practice.

"That was an amazing goal, Sam," Emily said.

"The amazing pass came first. Thank you."

"My pleasure," she said, bowing and laughing.

I started laughing, too. Playing was always fun, but winning was the cherry on top.

"See you at our place at five," I called to her as I joined my family.

"You won!" Zoe shouted.

"We did," I agreed.

Aiden gave my braid a tug. "Nice game, Triple S."

That was my family nickname (it stood for Samantha

Sophia Stevens), but Aiden hadn't called me that for a long time.

"I didn't think you were watching," I said, proud that he'd seen my winning goal.

"I was watching. You know—"

"Hey, Aiden!"

We turned to see three guys standing by the basketball court.

Aiden dropped my braid like it was on fire and moved away from me.

I felt my face turn red.

Now that he was in high school, Aiden didn't like talking to me in public anymore. And "public" could be the bus stop, the mall or even our own front yard.

Sometimes our own *kitchen* was too public for him.

It really hurt my feelings, but I didn't know how to tell him that.

I pretended I didn't care and caught up with Mom.

"Ignore it," she said, patting my shoulder. "He's a teenager."

"He's a jerk," I muttered.

"He's your *brother*," she said with a bit of a warning in her tone. Mom hated name-calling.

"I know, but I wish—"

"If wishes were nickels, we'd all be rich," she said with a little smile.

"If wishes were fishes, we'd eat them with chips," I answered like I always did.

"If wishes were kisses, I'd have chapped lips." She leaned over to give me a smooch on the cheek.

And that was all it took for me to forget about Aiden and my hurt feelings.

As we walked back to the van, Kate and Zoe collected red, orange and yellow maple leaves to make bouquets, and I told Mom about Coach's plan to choose a team captain.

"The C would go right here," I said, pointing to the spot on my jersey. "And I'd get to wear it for the whole season."

"Very impressive," Mom said, eyes twinkling.

"What's so funny?" I asked, hoping she didn't think I was kidding myself.

"Nothing." She put an arm around me. "I'm just picturing what a great captain you will be." She gave my shoulder a squeeze.

What a great captain I "will" be. That was one of the things I loved most about Mom. She believed I could do anything.

And so did I.

Chapter
TWO

I walked through our front door trying to decide what I wanted more: a hot, soapy shower or an ice-cold drink.

"I want two goals just for me next time," Kate said as she dumped her coat on the couch.

"I want three," Zoe said, dropping hers on top of it.

"That's a lot of goals," I told them.

"You can do it!" Zoe cheered, throwing a balled-up fist in the air.

"Just like you can hang up your coats," Mom said, coming in behind them. "Both of you, please." She glanced at the cleats I'd slipped off and the muddy socks on my feet.

"I know," I told her. "Laundry room."

Right after a pit stop in the kitchen.

A cold drink was what I needed. Lemonade, if we had some. With a handful of ice cubes.

Aiden hip-checked me as he flipped through yesterday's mail, which Mom had reminded him to get from the box. He made a judgment call on each envelope and flyer: "Boring . . . boring . . . bill . . . boring . . . two-for-one Big Macs . . . boring . . . discount laser eye surgery, like *that's* a good idea . . . bill . . . boring . . . yes!" He held up his *Pulse* music magazine for the world (well, me) to see.

"Can I get in there?" I asked, nodding toward the kitchen.

He stepped out of the way and I made my move on the fridge. When I swung the door open, I was greeted by the sight of just about everything a thirsty girl could want: apple juice, cranberry juice, a jug of ice-cold water.

And lemonade.

I poured myself a tall glass and chugged it without even closing the fridge. As soon as I was finished, I poured another and gulped some more.

"Wow," Mom said, dropping her canvas bag on the counter. "What is it with you and the drinks lately? Is it hot in here or something?"

I shrugged. "No, I'm just thirsty."

For the past week, my mouth felt like it had been

stuffed with cotton balls and then blasted with a hair dryer. Even worse than the dryness and thirst was the side effect: I spent a lot of time running back and forth to the bathroom. It was getting kind of embarrassing, especially at school.

"Save some for the rest of us," Mom said.

"I will," I told her, taking another gulp.

"And Samantha?"

"Yes?" I asked as I wiped my mouth with the sleeve of my jersey.

"Your next drink is water."

"Okay," I said, laughing.

"By the way, how's your room looking?"

I pictured the scene we'd left behind that morning.

"Uh . . ." Like we needed a professional cleanup crew.

"I need you and the girls to take care of it before dinner."

"But it's Saturday."

"And?"

"And Emily's coming over."

"All the more reason to tidy up," Mom said with a shrug. "Dinner's at five."

Just like every other day of my life. She didn't have to tell me that.

* * *

It didn't take too long for me to clean up my side of our room. I took the job seriously, hanging up pants, folding T-shirts and putting everything in its place. My sisters, on the other hand, piled everything in their closet and used their combined weight to push the door closed.

"Mom's going to figure that out," I told them.

The door looked like it could pop off its hinges at any second, causing an explosion of sequins, dresses and hundreds of stuffed animals. Not that I was going to wait around for that to happen.

"Where are you going?" Zoe asked as I pulled on leggings and my favorite sweatshirt, a hand-me-down from Aiden.

"Where do you think?" Kate asked her.

"To practice in the backyard," Zoe said, reciting the words she'd heard me say at least a thousand times before.

"Why do you even ask?" Kate asked, elbowing her.

Even though I'd already played today, I knew that if I wanted to be team captain, my playing would have to be sharper than ever. That meant even more practice.

"See you later," I called over my shoulder as I headed downstairs. When I got to the last four steps, I jumped the rest of the way, landing on the carpet with a satisfying thud.

I put on my old cleats and jogged outside, grabbing a ball and some cones from the garage. Once I'd set up my usual obstacle course, I was ready to start dribbling. I hung the stopwatch I'd gotten for my birthday around my neck, pushed the start button and took off.

I whipped around my course twice, as quickly as I could, keeping the ball nice and close so I wouldn't lose control on the turns.

By the time I'd finished, I was breathing hard, so I knew the drill was doing some good. I checked the stopwatch and saw that my time was just under a minute and a half. I took a deep breath and did it again, this time keeping the ball even closer.

One minute and twenty seconds.

Not bad.

"What are you doing?" Aiden asked from behind me.

I turned around. "What does it look like?" I asked, using his favorite question against him.

"Drills," he said, smiling.

"Then it's probably drills."

"Want some company?"

I smiled back, trying to remember the last time he'd offered. "Sure."

He took off his hoodie and dropped it on the ground. Now he was wearing a T-shirt for the same weird band I'd seen posters of in his room.

Aiden hummed as he adjusted my cones. I watched him, glad that he wanted to hang out with me for a change. "This is how Coach Barnard used to do it," he said as he moved the final cone into place.

I looked over the new course, which was tighter and trickier than mine. I already liked the challenge of it.

I rested one foot on top of my ball. "Do you miss it?" I asked.

"What? Soccer?" Aiden shoved his hands in the pockets of his baggy jeans. "No." He shrugged. "I mean, I don't know. Sometimes."

"You were *so* good," I said, meaning it. He used to keep his trophies on the bookshelf in his room, but they'd disappeared into a box under his bed when school started.

"I was okay," he mumbled, but we both knew that was a major understatement. He was awesome.

"Why'd you quit?" I'd been wanting to ask for ages.

He shrugged again and was quiet for a moment before he said, "None of my friends were playing soccer, so . . ."

"What do you mean? You had friends on the team."

"Yeah, but none of the guys from school play soccer."

"You mean they play other sports, like hockey or something?"

"Hockey? Logan and Caleb and those guys?" he asked, laughing. "Yeah, right."

"What about music? Are they in the school band?"

"No." He looked at me like I was crazy.

"So, what do they *do*?" I asked.

"Hang out, I guess. Play video games. Goof around." I must have made a face, because he said, "You'll know what I'm talking about when you get to high school."

I rolled my eyes. "You keep saying that."

"Because it's true. It's not like middle school, Sam. The kids are—"

"Boring?" I asked. It sure sounded like it to me.

"Nah," he said, shaking his head. "They're different. They care about different stuff."

I figured I'd never have a better chance, so I quietly asked, "Is that why you pretended you didn't know me today?"

At first he acted like he didn't know what I was talking about, but when I kept staring, he gave up. "You mean after the game?"

"Yeah, after the game when you walked away from me in the middle of a conversation." *Like I was nobody*, I wanted to add.

He winced. "Come on, Sam. I was just talking to the guys and—"

"I wasn't cool enough." Even though I'd just scored the winning goal for my team.

"It's not about being cool," he said. "It's just . . .

you're my little sister. None of the guys hang out with twelve-year-old girls."

"Then what were they doing at a twelve-year-old girls' soccer game?" I asked.

I could tell by the look on his face that he hadn't thought of that. "I think James has a sister or something," he muttered.

"He does. It's Kylie, and I'm pretty sure James was ignoring her, too. Do high school kids get extra credit for that or something?"

Aiden shook his head. "Look, I'm sorry, okay?"

I shrugged. "Fine."

"Don't be mad, Triple S."

"I'm not." And I wasn't. I was disappointed.

He'd always been my friend and my protector, and I didn't want that to change. But it wasn't up to me.

"Look, are we going to run these drills or not?" he asked, raising an eyebrow.

"Yeah," I said. "I need to play my best if I'm going to make team captain."

"Captain, huh?" He nodded. "I guess I can see that."

"Really?"

"Sure. You're the best forward on that team. Maybe even the best player."

Hearing those words was almost enough to make me forget how he'd acted at the game.

Okay, it *was* enough.

He might not have shown it all the time, but maybe my brother was still on my side when it mattered.

But just as I finished that thought, I heard the sound I'd learned to hate: a soft buzzing noise that came from the depths of Aiden's pocket.

He whipped out his phone and pushed a button. "What's up?"

I kept dribbling, waiting for him to finish the call so we could hang out. Instead, he picked up his hoodie and started walking back into the house.

"Busy? Nah," he said into the phone. "I'm not doing anything."

Suddenly, the backyard felt terribly empty.

* * *

I was setting the table for dinner when the doorbell rang.

Zoe ran downstairs like the house was on fire. "I'll get it!"

"It's just Emily," I called after her.

But as far as Zoe was concerned, there was no "just" when it came to my best friend. Emily had long, red hair and blue eyes, exactly like Ariel from *The Little Mermaid*.

"Hey, Z," Emily said as my sister swung the door open.

Suddenly, the biggest chatterbox in the house became the shyest, staring at my friend in awed silence.

"Are you going to let her in?" I called from the kitchen doorway.

Zoe stepped out of the way. As usual, she studied Emily's sneakers, just in case they were hiding fins instead of feet.

"Dinner should be ready in—" I started to say, just as Mom rang the dinner bell that hung next to the stove.

Our kitchen table went from empty to jam-packed in less than thirty seconds. That was the way the Stevens family operated, and we quickly fell into a natural rhythm.

Mom dished out pork chops and Dad passed the potatoes. I scooped some carrots onto my plate and handed the bowl to Emily, who traded me for a steaming plate of broccoli.

The second my plate was filled (with everything but the green beans I hated), I took a long drink of milk, draining half of my glass in one gulp. It tasted incredible! Cold, creamy and *so* refreshing.

As I stabbed a broccoli tree with my fork, the whole family was talking at once. As usual.

"Ask me to spell peanut butter," Kate said to anyone who might be listening.

"You promised to eat at least five carrots," Mom reminded her.

Kate spooned the smallest carrots she could find onto her plate.

"Are there mermaids in space?" Zoe asked Emily.

"Um . . ." Emily glanced at me. "I think they need water."

"There's no such thing as mermaids," Aiden answered.

"Very funny," Zoe said, sticking out her tongue.

"Seriously. They're pretend," he told her.

"No, *you're* pretend," she said, like that even made sense.

"Is there more milk?" I asked Mom.

"In the fridge," she said. "Just one glass, okay? Then you switch to water." She glanced at me. "I mean it."

I got up from my seat. "I can't help it if I'm super-thirsty."

"Isn't anyone going to ask me to spell peanut butter?"

"Fine," Aiden sighed and rolled his eyes. "Spell peanut butter."

"Can you please pass the meat?" Dad asked Mom.

"P . . . E . . . A—"

"I need more applesauce," Zoe said.

"Samantha, can you help her?" Mom asked.

I scooped some sauce out of the bowl for my sister.

"N . . . U—"

"Who's driving me to Caleb's tomorrow?" Aiden interrupted.

"The Number Seventeen," Mom told him.

"The bus?" he groaned. "I hate riding that thing. Only losers take the bus."

"I take the bus," I reminded him.

He nodded like I'd proven his point. "Mom, seriously. It's social suicide."

"If you don't like the bus, you could always walk," Dad suggested.

"Walk?" Aiden gasped.

"Yes." Dad grinned. "Place one foot in front of the other. You've been doing it since you were about a year old."

I smiled. I'd started at nine months.

"T . . . B . . . U—" Kate stopped and glared at most of the table. "No one's *listening.*"

"We all know how to spell it already," I told her.

"I don't," Zoe said, applesauce dripping down her chin.

"Maybe I can get a ride with Dominic," Aiden mumbled.

"Only if there's an adult in the car," Mom reminded him.

"But he has his licence!"

"Jason?" Mom asked Dad.

"He hasn't had it long enough, Aiden," Dad told him. "You know the rules."

"Hello?" Kate said. "Peanut butter?"

"No one cares about peanut butter, okay?" Aiden snapped.

"Watch your tone," Dad said.

"*You* care," Kate said, pointing at my brother. "You're the one who asked me to spell it, and now you're not even *listening*."

"Aiden," Mom warned when she saw the expression on his face.

"Fine." He sighed. "I'm listening."

Kate frowned and scrunched up her face. "I lost my place."

"Seriously?" Aiden groaned.

"Start again, honey," Mom said.

"I don't want to start the whole thing over," Kate whined.

"Oh, for crying out loud," Aiden said, rolling his eyes. "Spell jam."

"That's too easy." She folded her arms across her chest.

"I need more applesauce," Zoe said.

"I just gave you some," I told her.

Dad checked her plate. "Finish what you have first."

"Come on, you guys," Kate begged. "Something harder than jam."

"Almost everything is harder than jam," I told her. "It's practically liquid." Emily laughed.

"No, to *spell*," Kate said. "I need something harder than jam."

"How about rutabaga?" Emily suggested.

Kate frowned for a second, then silently mouthed the word a couple of times. "R . . . U?"

"Being driven crazy?" Aiden asked. "Yes, I am."

"Very funny," Kate snapped.

"I think that's enough spelling for now," Dad told her.

"And that's enough milk, Samantha," Mom said as I emptied my glass again.

"I know," I told her. I got up to get some water.

Chapter
THREE

After dinner, Emily and I helped Dad do the dishes before we headed upstairs. The plan was to do some work on our social studies project, and then Emily would sleep over.

"I wish I lived here," my friend said.

"Believe me, you don't," I told her. "The whole place is crazy."

I proved the point when I opened my bedroom door. The view almost knocked me over.

"Are you kidding me?" I gasped at my sisters. "When did you have time to do this?"

Almost every board game, puzzle and deck of cards we owned was out of hiding and spread across the floor.

"What?" Kate asked.

"We just cleaned this up!" I choked.

"No," she said, shaking her head. "We cleaned up all the clothes and stuff." She pointed to the closet door, still barely holding all the junk in. "Remember?"

I groaned. "Of course, I remember. But we didn't put it away so you could make *another* huge mess."

"It's only on the floor," Zoe reasoned. She smiled at Emily.

"Seriously," I told them. "You need to get this stuff out of the way."

"But we're still playing with it," Kate argued.

"All of it?" I raised an eyebrow. "Candy Land, Snakes and Ladders, memory, dominoes, old maid *and* checkers?"

"Uh-huh," Kate said, sounding a little less sure.

"Put it away," I said, doing my best impression of Mom when she meant business.

"You're a party pooper," Kate moaned.

"Yeah. Party pooper," Zoe echoed, like she always did.

"Anyway, it's *my* stuff," Kate said.

"Yeah, well it's *our* room," I reminded her.

"So?" Kate demanded.

"Yeah, so?" Zoe echoed.

"So, do you want me to bring Mom in on this?"

"No!" they shrieked.

While they whipped around the room, loading game

boxes with a thousand parts and pieces, Emily and I got settled at my desk and started on our project.

"Ancient Egypt." She smiled as she twisted the end of her red ponytail around her fingers. "I'd like to go there someday."

"*Ancient* Egypt?" I giggled. "Do you have a time machine you haven't told me about?"

She rolled her eyes. "I mean *today's* Egypt. Don't you think it would be cool to see the Sphinx or the Great Pyramids?"

"Cruise the Nile and ride a camel?" I asked. "Definitely."

Emily frowned. "I don't know about *that*. Camels are supposed to be kind of mean."

"I can handle mean," I told her. "I live with Aiden, remember?"

She laughed. "So, where do we start?"

I was really glad I had my best friend for a partner. I could suggest anything and she'd never tell me it was a bad or dumb idea. "I think we should do our project on the pyramids. We could talk about how they were built and why. Maybe make a poster?"

She thought for a couple of seconds, then smiled. "We should *build* a pyramid."

"Ooh, that would be cool," I said. "I bet Ms. Handel would love a model."

Emily tapped her pen against her forehead. "Hey, since it's an oral report, maybe we could dress in costumes."

"Be a mermaid," Zoe suggested as she dumped a bunch of dominoes into a checkers box.

"They didn't have mermaids in Ancient Egypt," I told her. Of course, they didn't have them *anywhere*, but I wasn't going to bring that up.

"Hey, Emily," Kate said. "Ask me to spell elephant."

Emily grinned at me, then looked back at Kate. "Okay, spell elephant."

My sister put her hands at her sides, like she was in a competition, and slowly spelled the word.

"Good job," Emily said, clapping.

"Ask me another one."

"We're trying to work here, Kate," I told her.

"Come on," she whined. "Just one more."

"Ask yourself," I told her. "And, really you guys need to play somewhere else."

"Fine." Kate leaned in closer to me and whispered, "If you give me some candy."

"Yeah, right. I don't have any candy."

She sniffed the air in front of my face. "You smell like candy."

How weird did they have to act when I had a friend over? "Can you guys, please, just go downstairs?"

"Why?" Kate asked, arms folded across her chest.

"Uh, so you won't be *upstairs*? Like I said, we're trying to work here."

"Whatever," Kate sighed, heading for the door.

"Whatever," Zoe repeated, following her.

"I need my own room," I muttered once the door was closed. "Sorry about that."

"They're cute," Emily said. When she saw the expression on my face she laughed. "Okay, annoying, but cute."

"So, back to the pyramid model." I said. "What if we made it out of brownies?"

"That would be awesome," she said, grinning. "We could use frosting for the glue."

"And the class can eat it after we finish the report."

She grinned even more. "Wait. Maybe we should use blondies instead."

"What's a blondie?"

"It's like a butterscotch brownie. They're kind of a tan color instead of brown."

"Genius! And we can sprinkle brown sugar around the bottom, like sand."

I was pretty sure we were on our way to acing what had suddenly become a delicious project.

Blondies. I couldn't wait.

* * *

We made some decent progress on the project for an hour or so, and then Mom called upstairs, "We've got popcorn and a movie if anyone's interested!"

"I could handle some popcorn," Emily said.

"But can you handle your mini-stalker watching you instead of the movie?"

She glanced at me. "It isn't *The Little Mermaid*, is it?"

"No," I said, laughing.

"Good. I don't want to relive that experience anytime soon."

I knocked on Aiden's door as we passed it. "Are you watching the movie?"

"I'm on the phone!" he barked.

"Wow," Emily whispered, following me downstairs. "Nice attitude."

"Tell me about it."

Once we were settled on the big couch, covered in blankets and propped up by soft pillows, everything was perfect. The popcorn was buttery, the pop was ice-cold and the movie was a funny comedy. Sure, it stunk that Aiden wanted to hang out in his gloomy room instead of watching it with us, but it was fun to laugh and joke around with everyone else.

Zoe and Kate fell asleep before the movie ended, and when Mom and Dad carried them upstairs, they told me and Emily not to stay up too late.

We didn't last much longer than they had. When neither of us could get through a sentence without yawning, we decided to go to bed.

"Sam?" Emily whispered from my top bunk.

"Yeah?"

"I think you're going to be team captain."

"Really?" I asked, excited until I ran through the competition in my head. "But Kylie's our leading scorer." And she wasn't shy about reminding everyone of that, including Coach.

"So?" Emily asked.

"So, we win games by scoring goals. If she scores more goals, she's more . . . valuable than me."

"That's totally not true, Sam. You're one of the best players we have, but you're also, like, the heart of the team."

I realized she was just trying to make me feel good, and I should be doing the same thing for her.

"I think you have a good chance, too." And she did. Emily was a strong player.

"I doubt it," she said, but I could hear the smile in her voice. "Anyway, I just want you to know I'll be happy for you when you get picked."

"*If*," I corrected. "I'll be happy for you, too," I told her, hoping I really would. I wanted it so much; it was hard to imagine congratulating someone else. Even Emily.

The last thing I thought of before I fell asleep was the white C on my jersey.

Team captain.

If Coach picked me, it would be the best thing that had ever happened to me.

* * *

That night I had a terrible sleep, filled with all kinds of creepy dreams. I woke up a couple of times with my heart racing. When I checked the clock and saw that it was only three and then four-thirty in the morning, I rolled over and made myself fall asleep again.

When I woke up for real the next morning, the sun was warm on my face. I stretched my whole body, like our cat Tony, and smiled.

I started to climb out of bed, and that's when I noticed something was wrong.

When I moved my blankets, cold air slipped under them.

Super-cold air.

I curled my legs toward my stomach, trying to find a warm spot, but my pajama bottoms felt weird. It took a second or two to realize that they were *wet*.

I sat up and threw off my comforter.

There was a dark circle on my pajamas, and when I jumped off the mattress, I saw that my bottom sheet was wet, too.

No way.

I gulped.

I'd wet the bed?

I couldn't believe it! I was twelve years old and I'd wet my bed like a little kid.

I could feel my face burning as I glanced up at the top bunk. Emily's eyes were still closed, which was a total relief.

What would she think if she saw what I'd done? I'd seriously die of embarrassment if *anyone* found out.

I peeked at Kate and Zoe, letting out my breath when I saw that they were still sleeping, too. I was really glad they hadn't crawled into bed with me during the night like they sometimes did.

I looked back at my sheets.

I'd wet the bed?

Even Zoe didn't have "accidents" anymore.

I was so freaked out about it, I almost started to cry. I squeezed my eyes shut until I was sure I wouldn't.

I shouldn't have had so much to drink before bed! That had to be it. All of that milk and water with dinner. A Coke during the movie. It was my own stupid fault.

I glanced at Tony on my bed, purring in his sleep. But Clyde, the stuffed giraffe I'd had since I was a baby, was staring at me with his googly eyes. Luckily, he was the only witness; I wouldn't have to worry about him talking.

As quickly and quietly as I could, I stripped the sheets off my bed, relieved that the mattress pad underneath them was still clean and dry. It must have happened right before I woke up, and the liquid hadn't had a chance to soak through. I balled up the sheets so the wet parts wouldn't show and carried them into the bathroom where I dumped them on the floor. I peeled off my pajamas and added them to the soggy pile.

Gross.

I got into the shower, washed my hair, then used at least half a bar of soap to clean myself up. When I finally felt normal again, I got out, dried off, put on my robe and carried the laundry downstairs. I wanted to throw it in the washing machine before anyone else was up.

I hadn't counted on Mom being in the kitchen so early.

"Good morning," she said as I walked in. She was drinking a cup of coffee and reading the newspaper.

"Hi," I said, hurrying past her and wishing she was still in her bedroom.

If wishes were nickels, we'd all be rich.

If wishes were fishes, we'd eat them with—

"You're doing laundry?" Mom asked, interrupting the thought.

"Just trying to help out," I said, feeling my cheeks get hot from the lie.

She didn't look like she believed me. "Well . . . thank you. I'm going to do a load of colors, so if you want to leave those with the whites—"

"I'll just throw them in," I said quickly.

"But you don't have a full load. Let's wait for your sisters to get up, and we'll do all of your sheets together."

"No!" I practically shouted. "I mean," I said, trying to get control of myself, "I'll just do a small load."

Mom shook her head and started to smile. "Okay, I guess. Thanks for the help, honey."

I carried the load into the laundry room and dropped it into the washer. When I measured out the detergent, I added a little extra, just to be on the safe side.

Once I'd turned the dial and heard the first splash of water, I could breathe again.

That was way too close a call.

When I got back to the bedroom, Emily was yawning and stretching, just like I'd done. "Where'd you go?"

"To the bathroom."

She squinted at me. "You already had a shower?"

I nodded. "I thought we could kick the ball around a little before breakfast."

"Cool," she said.

Whew!

When I turned toward the closet, Kate was standing in front of me, blocking the way.

"Where are you hiding them?" she demanded.

I gulped, thinking about my sheets. I didn't want *anyone* to know what had happened, and that included my sisters.

"Hiding what?" I asked.

She rolled her eyes. "The candies."

That again? "What candies?" I asked her, getting exasperated.

"Come on, Samantha."

"I seriously don't know what you're talking about."

She stepped closer and sniffed me. "Yup. Fruity, like strawberries. I can *smell* candy on you."

"Well, I can *smell* crazy on you," I told her. "I swear I don't have any."

She scowled at me, like she was trying to decide whether to believe me or not. "I'm watching you," she warned.

It was my turn to roll my eyes. "Halloween's coming up. You'll be neck-deep in candy soon, anyway."

"Are you trick-or-treating with us?" Zoe asked hopefully.

"No. Emily and I are going together. Right, Em?"

"Yeah. This will probably be our last year."

"Why?" Kate asked, surprised.

Emily shrugged. "We're getting too old for trick-or-treating."

Of course, we were too old for wetting the bed, too.

But I didn't want to think about that. It was a one-time deal. An accident. It would never happen again.

Chapter
FOUR

At lunch on Tuesday, Mai and I snagged the Strikers' favorite table in the cafeteria and waited for the rest of the team to join us.

"How'd you do on that math test?" she asked, biting into a quesadilla.

"Seventy-six. What about you?"

"Eighty-three."

"Nice!"

"It was harder than I thought it would be."

"Me, too," I told her as Emily and Kylie sat down.

"This has been the longest day of my life," Kylie groaned.

"It's only noon," I pointed out, laughing. She was always dramatic.

"Exactly." She pulled a yogurt from her lunch bag and groaned again. "Yuck! My mom knows I hate the peach ones."

"I've got fruit gummies," Mai said.

"Not fair," Kylie told her.

"So, Alyssa's going to miss practice tonight," Emily announced.

"Bad idea when Coach is choosing a captain," Mai said, shaking her head.

"It's her dad's birthday," Emily explained. "And I don't think she wants to be captain."

I couldn't imagine anyone *not* wanting the job.

Kylie shrugged. "Coach wouldn't have picked her, anyway."

"Why not?" I asked.

"Because it's totally between us."

"Who?" Emily asked.

"Me and Sam," Kylie said, like it was a fact.

I glanced at my best friend, who didn't seem offended at all.

"What about Emily?" I suggested. "Brianne or Sara?"

"Mmm, I don't think so," Kylie said, shaking her head.

"She's right," Mai agreed. "You guys are the two best players on the team."

I tried to concentrate on the conversation after that, but I kept daydreaming about Coach picking me.

I was going to have to do my absolute best at every practice and game. I couldn't give her a single reason not to choose me.

* * *

But after dinner that night, when Mom said it was time to leave for practice, the strangest thing happened. I didn't want to go.

For no reason at all, I was totally wiped out. In fact, I would have rather stayed home and napped than play my favorite sport.

It was crazy, and it had never, *ever* happened before.

When we got to the field, Mom parked the car. Then she looked at me and rested a hand on my forehead to check my temperature. "Are you feeling okay?"

"Yeah, I'm just tired." Totally exhausted, actually, but tired took less energy to say.

"You've been tired a lot lately."

"I know. I'm actually tired of being tired," I tried to joke.

"Maybe an early bedtime tonight?"

I nodded. Usually I would have argued, hoping to stay up and watch TV or read. But that day all I wanted was to get through practice so I could go home and sleep for, like, two whole days. Maybe three.

It was tempting to curl up and doze off right there in the passenger seat.

But I had to practice.

Before I left, I opened the glove compartment, hoping there was a leftover granola bar or something in there. My stomach was growling. Again.

"What are you looking for?" Mom asked.

"A snack."

"You just ate dinner," she said, shaking her head. "Two helpings, if I remember correctly."

I shrugged. "You do remember correctly, but I'm still hungry."

"Tired and hungry? I've said it before: this has got to be a growth spurt in the works."

"As I've said before, that would be nice." I was one of the shortest girls on the team, and even though speed and endurance were what counted, a little height couldn't hurt.

"I'll see you after practice," Mom said.

I kissed her cheek and climbed out of the car.

I started walking toward my teammates, who were talking on the sidelines. They were waiting for the boys' team to finish its practice. We shared the space, which was fine, except when the boys took too long.

As I reached my team, I noticed my mouth was dried out again. Geez. We wouldn't have our Gatorade until we took a break halfway through practice, so I dug into Coach Donaldson's cooler and found a bottle of water. I chugged it in about three gulps.

"Wow. Thirsty much?" Kylie asked me.

I swallowed the last drop. "Yeah, super-thirsty."

Even worse? I had to go to the bathroom (*again*), but there was nowhere to go. Soccer practice wasn't like camping at the coast where all you needed was a bush and a little sister on lookout duty.

Coach blew her whistle and waved to the boys' coach to let him know we were ready to get started.

I almost grabbed another drink, but if a whole bottle of water hadn't killed my thirst, would another one make a difference? Probably not.

I ignored my dry mouth, and my full bladder, as we stretched and then ran laps. By the time we got started on our drills, I'd managed to forget about both.

That's the thing about soccer. It makes me forget everything but dribbling, passing and taking shots on goal. It doesn't matter how bad my day's been, or how tired I feel, the second I step on the field, all I want to do is play.

Hoping to make a good impression, I volunteered to help Coach Donaldson set up cones.

"Thanks, Sam," she said, handing me a stack of little orange triangles.

"No problem."

"Let's do five straight rows, toward the far goal. Ten cones per row."

After I'd finished, I joined the rest of the Strikers to line up. When my turn came, I made sure I hustled like never before.

Team captain, here I come!

* * *

The rest of the school week passed in a blur, and I went to bed early Friday night, determined to get at least eight hours of solid sleep.

And I did. But when I woke up on Saturday morning, I still felt kind of tired. And kind of sick, actually.

The walk to the bathroom felt like a hike (partly because of the piles of stuffed animals I had to climb over) and it took me minutes of standing under the hot water to really wake up. And that was weird because it was *game day*, my favorite day of the week.

I tried to shake it off, remembering that I'd felt the same way before practice.

I got over it then. I'll get over it again.

The Strikers were the home team, so I put my jersey on green-side out. When I was dressed, I looked at myself in the mirror and imagined the C above my heart. It was going to look perfect.

Too bad I didn't.

There were dark bags under my eyes, like I hadn't slept at all.

I shook out my arms and jumped up and down a

few times, hoping to get my blood and energy flowing. Coach wasn't going to pick a team captain who was dragging on the field.

"Come on, Samantha," I whispered, to my reflection. "Get it together."

But I couldn't.

From the second I joined Emily and the rest of the team, I was lagging behind. My laps were slower than usual, my dribbling was sloppy, and when I took practice shots, they didn't have any power behind them.

I had no oomph, as Dad would say.

Nobody noticed during the warm-ups, but it was a different story when the ref blew her whistle to start the game.

Kylie passed the ball to me, and I dribbled toward the far goal. I wasn't moving as fast as I usually did, and the next thing I knew, one of the Firebirds stole the ball.

I turned to run after her, but couldn't catch up.

My heart dropped down into my cleats when I saw her take a shot on our goal and score.

A bunch of the Strikers sighed and groaned.

"It's okay," Emily called out to our teammates, clapping her hands. "It's just one goal and it's still early."

"Sorry, guys," I said. "I'm still waking up, I guess."

"Don't worry about it," Alyssa said. "We'll get it back."

"Are you okay?" Emily asked me quietly.

"Just tired," I told her. And embarrassed to have let the team down less than thirty seconds into the game.

From that moment on, I pushed myself as hard as I could, trying to make up for it.

Of course, I knew that we all make rotten plays now and then, and anyone can have a bad day. The team wasn't mad at me or anything, but I still wanted to shine out there.

By halftime, I hadn't scored a single goal, and I felt tired enough to have played two full games.

As I walked over to the sideline, Kylie jogged past me.

"Good job out there," I called after her.

"Thanks," she said over her shoulder. "But I can't do it *all*, you know."

What was that supposed to mean? And why did she have to say it when Coach was so close?

"Nice playing, girls," Coach said, passing around the oranges.

I grabbed a couple of slices and a bottle of water.

It seemed like only a minute had passed before the ref blew her whistle to start the second half.

Already?

"Samantha, do you need a longer break?" Coach Donaldson asked, looking concerned.

"No!"

"You seem a bit—"

"I'm fine," I told her. "I'm great, actually."

The last thing I wanted was for Coach to think I was tired out. A team captain needs to have a ton of energy.

I was relieved when she sent me back in, but the relief didn't last for long.

No matter how many times the rest of the Strikers passed me the ball, I just couldn't pull it together.

By the end of the game (which we lost by two goals), I was hot, sweaty, exhausted and *angry*.

"Want to sleep over tonight?" Emily asked, once we'd congratulated the Firebirds on their win. "We can bake cookies and watch scary movies."

Any other day I would have rushed over to ask Mom for permission, but after my performance, I just wanted to be alone.

"I can't."

"Oh, okay," she said, looking surprised. "Maybe next weekend."

"Sure," I said, doing my best to smile like nothing was wrong. But who was I kidding? I sighed. "I can't believe how rotten I played, Em."

She shook her head, and her red ponytail swished back and forth. "Don't worry about it. You had *one* bad game."

"But at the worst possible time. I wanted to show Coach Donaldson my skills and I blew it."

"You didn't blow anything, Sam. She already knows how good you are."

"You think so?"

"Sam, *everybody* knows how good you are."

That made me feel a bit better. And she was right. One bad game after a ton of good ones wasn't a big deal. And Coach Donaldson wasn't the kind of person who would hold one crummy performance against me.

"Tough game," Mom said when I met up with her and my sisters on the sideline.

"Yeah."

"How come you kept missing?" Zoe asked.

I felt my cheeks get hot. "I don't know."

"You used to be really good."

"I still am," I told her through gritted teeth.

"Not today," Kate said.

"Thanks a lot," I muttered.

"Girls," Mom said. "Leave her alone."

We walked without saying anything for a little bit. I tried not to feel frustrated, but I couldn't help it.

What was wrong with me?

"I stunk," I finally said to Mom, looking at the ground.

"That might be pushing it." She laid one hand on my shoulder. "But I must say you didn't seem like your usual self out there today. Are you feeling okay?"

I nodded as we reached the van. I was still quiet when I'd climbed in and buckled my seat belt. I'd blown every chance I'd had at scoring, and I'd been outrun and outplayed from start to finish.

I really had stunk.

And I hated it.

"Samantha?" Mom said.

"Yes?"

"You keep licking your lips. I have Chapstick in my purse if you want some."

"I'm just thirsty," I told her. "I'll have some water when we get home."

And before I knew it, we were parked in the driveway and my sisters were already halfway up our front steps. I'd fallen asleep.

"What time did you go to bed last night?" Mom asked.

"I don't know." I rubbed at my eyelids. They felt like they were weighed down by rocks. "Nine o'clock?"

"Did you stay up reading?"

"No," I said through a yawn. "I went right to sleep."

But I had gotten up to pee three times.

"You must be coming down with something. I think it's time for a nap, Samantha."

I was too tired to argue.

Chapter
FIVE

On Monday morning, something terrible happened.
Again.

"You've got to be kidding me," I whispered when I woke up to a familiar cold, wet feeling.

I pulled back my comforter and saw another dark spot on my flowered sheets. I groaned, then froze. I held my breath and listened for a few seconds. I couldn't hear anything but deep breathing and snoring around me.

Whew! Kate and Zoe were asleep.

That was lucky, but I still needed to get the sheets into the wash before Mom got up. I'd have to move fast!

As silently as possible, I changed out of my wet pajama bottoms and into some black leggings that were lying by my desk. I yanked off the sheets as quickly and quietly as I could, checking over my shoulder every few seconds to make sure no one was watching me.

The only eyes that met mine were Tony the tabby's

golden ones. He gave me a curious look for a second or two then started licking his paw, ignoring me.

I took a deep breath.

How could I have wet the stupid bed again? I'd barely had anything to drink the night before.

I rolled the sheets and the wet mattress pad into a ball.

"What are you doing?" Kate asked, her voice croaking in her throat.

I gulped. "Nothing. Go back to sleep."

My heart pounded as I hurried down the stairs, trying not to step on the creaky ones.

Mom was in the kitchen! How was I going to explain my sudden interest in laundry?

I had to hide the sheets, but where?

Panic started to build in my chest.

I glanced at the hall closet, but knew it wouldn't work. People were in and out of there all day, grabbing coats or shoes.

I thought about the cupboard under the stairs, but it was right next to the heating vent. The minute those sheets dried out, they'd stink up the whole house.

I was running out of options.

Then I heard a loud rumbling outside and started to smile. What were the chances?

It was garbage day!

My heart beat even faster as I clutched the sheets with one hand and pulled a pair of Aiden's sneakers out of the closet with the other.

I heard some more rattling in the kitchen and knew I only had a minute to fix the mess I was in.

The front door hinges squeaked a little when I gently pulled the door open, but not loud enough for Mom to hear. I slipped out onto the front porch and hustled down the steps.

Quick! Quick! Quick!

The garbage truck was just two houses away. The timing was absolutely perfect!

I ran the length of the driveway like an Olympic sprinter and lifted the garbage can lid. There was just enough room left for the balled-up linens.

Everything was going my way!

I shoved the sheets and pad inside, pushed the lid closed and scooted back toward the house.

When I was inside, I closed the door and leaned against it, totally overwhelmed with relief.

No one would know I'd wet the bed.

I was safe.

I slipped Aiden's shoes off and tucked them back into the closet.

Since I didn't have the sheets to worry about anymore, my brain switched to the real issue.

Why was I wetting the bed? I'd never had any problems before, but suddenly I'd done it twice?

It was obvious that I needed to change something, and on the way upstairs, I came up with a plan. All I needed to do was stop drinking right after dinner. Not even a sip after seven o'clock, no matter how much I wanted one (and most of the time, I really, really wanted one).

I could stick to that plan, especially if it meant no more cold, wet morning surprises.

I headed straight for the bathroom and undressed for the shower. That's when I noticed something weird. The leggings I'd hurried to put on weren't black. They were navy blue.

And I didn't own any navy blue leggings.

I picked them up off the floor and held them up to my waist. In my big rush, I hadn't noticed how short they were.

I peeked at the tag in the waistband and saw they were a size eight.

I was a twelve.

Kate was an eight.

How the heck had I fit into my little sister's pants?

Sure, they had an elastic waist, but seriously? A size eight?

I stood in the middle of the bathroom, trying to

figure it out. Yes, some of my clothes *had* been feeling loose lately, but I'd assumed I'd stretched my favorites out by wearing them too much.

Was it something else?

Curious, I stepped onto the scale and waited for the red numbers to appear.

Whoa!

I was ten pounds lighter than the last time I'd checked, and that was months ago.

How crazy was that?

I stepped off the scale and stared at myself in the mirror. I didn't think I looked any different.

I'd been eating a ton of food, to the point where Dad kept asking me if I was filling a hollow leg with steak and mashed potatoes.

And I'd *lost* weight? That didn't make sense.

None of it made sense.

But I couldn't ask anybody about it. If Mom or Coach found out that something was wrong with me, I'd probably have to kiss team captain goodbye.

No. I'd deal with it myself. I'd just have to eat more.

I started the shower, and while I scrubbed my skin and washed my hair, I tried to pretend that everything was normal.

* * *

When I was dressed and ready for school, I walked

back down to the kitchen. I was the only one there, so I set the table for cereal and put out the bowl of Mom's fresh fruit salad. I filled the milk and juice jugs and made sure everything was ready for the Stevens family's frantic morning meal.

Then I started to wonder where Mom had disappeared to.

I walked toward the stairs just as she was coming down.

"What's going on, Samantha?" she asked, looking confused.

I pointed toward the kitchen. "Nothing. The table's set and—"

"Where are your sheets?" she demanded. "And what's on your mattress?"

Oh, no!

I'd been so busy getting rid of the sheets and the mattress pad, I hadn't even thought about the mattress itself. I should have covered it with . . . something. *Anything.*

"What?" I asked, trying to buy some time.

"Why is your mattress *wet*, Samantha?" she asked, sounding less confused and more irritated.

I leaned toward the stairs and tilted my ear up, like I'd heard something. "She's coming!" I turned back to my mom. "Zoe needs you."

"She can wait until we sort this out."

"Uh . . . I have to go to the bathroom," I said, turning away. As I passed the stairs, I shouted, "I know, Zoe. She's coming!"

"What?" I heard my little sister shout from upstairs.

I ignored her and slipped into the bathroom. I could hear Mom sigh as she headed back upstairs.

I took a deep breath and stared in the mirror, wondering how I was going to explain my missing sheets and mattress pad to Mom. I didn't like keeping secrets from her, but wetting the bed was so embarrassing. There was no way I could tell her the truth.

I reached over to flush the toilet, then I ran the tap.

What was I going to say to her?

I needed to get out of the house and away from Mom's questions. I slipped out of the bathroom and grabbed my backpack from the kitchen. I opened the pantry, looking for a granola bar or something I could eat on the run.

"She didn't call me," Mom said from behind me.

I wasn't fast enough!

"Oh," I said, trying to smile. "I must have been hearing things."

Before Mom could say anything else, my sisters appeared in the kitchen. I'd never been so happy to see them, especially when they sat down at the table and started arguing about who got to pour their cereal first. The racket should have been enough to distract Mom, but it wasn't.

"Where are they?" she asked me.

"What?" I asked, trying to look innocent.

"Your sheets, Samantha. And your mattress pad. They're gone."

"They are?" I asked, widening my eyes and hoping I looked surprised.

Mom folded her arms. "They aren't in the laundry room, the linen cupboard or on your bed. What's going on?"

I realized the situation was hopeless. I took a deep breath and told her, "I threw them away."

"What?" she gasped.

I couldn't look at her face, so I focused on my hands. "I—"

"Look at me," she practically growled.

I glanced upward, saw how mad she was and looked back at my hands.

"Uh-oh," Zoe whispered.

"She's in big trouble," Kate whispered back.

"Big trouble," Zoe echoed.

"You two, upstairs," Mom said.

"But we just—"

"*Upstairs*," Mom said again.

They scrambled out of the room, and I wished I was right behind them.

"Look at me," Mom said again. She sounded almost as mad as she'd been the time Aiden stole a pack of gum from the grocery store.

My eyes met hers and a cold shiver went down my spine.

"Why?" she asked.

What was I supposed to say? There was no *good* explanation for what I'd done.

"I, uh . . . spilled some juice on them," I lied, knowing how strict my parents were about no snacks and drinks upstairs.

"Spilled some juice?"

"I know we aren't supposed to—"

She looked at me like I was crazy. "It would have washed out."

"I panicked, Mom."

She stared at me for a few seconds without saying a word, then finally asked, "Do you think your dad and I are made of money?"

"No," I said, swallowing hard. I'd heard them talk about bills before, plenty of times. I'd watched Mom organize her coupons for grocery shopping. I'd worn some of Aiden's hand-me-downs, then handed them down to Kate, who handed them down to Zoe.

"And yet you *threw away* perfectly good sheets for

no good reason? Do you have any idea what they cost? And the mattress pad?"

"A lot?" I asked quietly.

"A lot more than I want to spend right now," she said. "And that mattress is almost brand new, Samantha. I expect you to clean it up, and if there's even a hint of a stain—"

"Okay," I whispered, wishing I could tell her I wasn't the horrible, rule-breaking, juice-drinking, wasteful person she thought I was. But I'd chosen a lie, and I was stuck with it.

She stared at me like she'd never seen me before. "What on earth were you thinking?"

"What's going on?" Dad said from the doorway.

Mom told him what I'd done, and I braced myself for his reaction.

He sighed and rubbed his forehead. "Don't we have a pretty hard-and-fast rule about no food or drinks in the bedrooms?"

"Yes, but listen," I began, trying to come up with a way to smooth things over.

"No, *you* listen," Mom interrupted.

"I—"

"Not another word," she said, and I could hear the warning in her voice. "I don't like what's going on here, Samantha. First you break the rules, and then you sneak around trying to get rid of the evidence."

"But Mom—"

"I see no option but a punishment."

I gulped. Would she stop me from sleeping over at Emily's? Make me babysit Kate and Zoe? Would she—

"No soccer for a week."

"What?" I gasped, feeling all of the air leave my body. *No soccer?*

"You heard me," Mom said firmly. "No practices and no game this week."

Would she really do that to me? Take away the most important thing in my entire life? Just like that?

"But I can't miss a whole week!"

"You will," Mom said, crossing her arms.

I looked to Dad to help me out. He knew how much the Strikers meant to me. He had to fix this. He just *had to.*

"Dad, I—"

He shook his head. "I'm sorry, Mom's right."

"But Dad, you guys . . . Coach Donaldson is choosing a team captain soon!"

If my rotten playing in the last game hadn't been enough to ruin my dreams, missing practices and another game would do it. I felt sick to my stomach.

"Too bad," Mom said.

"No, you don't understand! If I miss a whole week—"

"If?" Mom asked. "You *are* missing a whole week. End of discussion."

And she walked out of the room.

"Dad?"

"Breaking the rules and sneaking around?" Dad said quietly. "I don't understand it."

"It was a mistake, Dad. A stupid one. But a whole week of soccer? Maybe you can talk to Mom and—"

"No," he said. "I'm sorry."

But he wasn't nearly as sorry as I was.

My hands were shaking as I pictured Coach giving that beautiful white C to someone else.

What had I done?

Chapter
SIX

I was late getting to my locker, so I didn't catch Emily before school started. I had to sit through my morning classes, totally freaking out, until lunchtime.

I broke my horrible news to my best friend while she ate a ham sandwich. For the first time in forever I wasn't hungry. I just played with my carrot sticks.

"So, no matter how much I begged, they said I couldn't play." I sighed, wishing more than anything that I'd never wet the stupid bed.

If wishes were nickels, we'd all be rich.

"Hold on," Emily said. "You're going to miss a whole week?"

I nodded. "Right when Coach is trying to choose a team captain."

"Yeah, but . . ." She shook her head. "That's not the most important thing."

"What?" She had to be kidding!

"I get that you're worried about making captain, but we need you on the field if we're going to win on Saturday."

I hadn't thought about that. We were up against the Storm, who had an almost perfect record.

What was I supposed to do while my teammates were playing their hearts out? Watch from the sidelines? Would Mom and Dad even let me go to the game?

"I need soccer," I murmured.

"Maybe if you talked to Coach—"

"I don't think she'll understand."

"I can't believe this is happening." Emily took a bite of her sandwich and looked thoughtful as she chewed.

"Me, neither." I jabbed a straw into my juice box about ten times harder than I needed to.

"Maybe your mom will change her mind," Emily said hopefully.

"You didn't see her face. There's no way."

"But she knows how important soccer is to you."

"It's my *life*. That's exactly why she chose this punishment."

She was quiet for a minute, then asked, "What did you do that was so bad, anyway?"

I shook my head. "Something stupid. I don't really want to talk about it."

"Oh." She looked hurt.

As much as I hated keeping secrets from Mom, I couldn't remember keeping *anything* from Emily before. She was my best friend and I trusted her completely, but this was different.

Nobody was going to find out what had really happened.

Ever.

* * *

When I got home from school that afternoon, all I wanted was to be alone. Unfortunately, Kate and Zoe were pretending to be princesses in our bedroom, Aiden was watching a zombie show on TV and Mom was in the kitchen making dinner.

I wasn't ready to face her.

There was only one place I could hope to be by myself, so I went upstairs to the bathroom, locked the door and filled the tub with hot water and bubbles. As I lowered myself into the bath, I hoped like crazy no one would interrupt me.

And they didn't. For about twenty seconds, anyway.

"Sam?" Zoe called through the door. "Are you in there?"

"I'm taking a bath!" I called out.

"Can I come in?"

I groaned. "Not right now, okay?"

"Just for a minute?"

Zoe, come on.

"Kate kicked me out of the castle."

"You're a princess, so it's your castle, too."

"She says she's a queen now, and she's in charge."

Was I really having this conversation? "Just tell her to let you back in, Zoe."

"Why can't I come in there?" she sniffled.

"Because I want to be alone."

"But I'm alone and I *hate* it."

I could tell from years of experience that she was getting close to a meltdown. I closed my eyes for a second, then climbed halfway out of the tub to unlock the door.

"Goody!" she said, stepping inside. She was wearing a puffy, pink dress and a tiara with pink plastic gems all over it.

"Lock the door behind you," I told her.

She did, and then she turned toward me, smiling like she'd won the lottery.

I had to admit, knowing she was so glad to hang out with me made me feel pretty good. She sat on the stool next to the tub and admired the mountain of bubbles that covered me.

"Why is Mom mad at you?" she asked.

"I did something I shouldn't have."

"You said a bad word?"

"No."

"You broke her special dish?"

"No." That was the last thing Zoe had done to get in trouble.

"Did you—"

"It doesn't matter what I did, okay?" I could tell by the look on her face she wanted to argue the point, so I asked, "Do you want to stay in here or not?"

I was relieved when she nodded.

She was quiet for less than ten seconds before she asked, "So, now you can't play soccer anymore?"

"Not forever, but this week."

"Even the game?" she gasped.

"Yes."

She crossed her arms over her chest. "Mom's mean."

I sighed. "Not really. She had to punish me somehow."

"But she's punishing *me*! Soccer games are my favorite."

"Mine, too." My absolute favorite thing in the world.

* * *

After my bath, Zoe went to look for a snack while I headed for our bedroom. It was still a mess, but empty for a change. I sat down at my desk and tried to concentrate on my homework, but I ended up staring out the window instead.

I was going to have to tell the rest of the Strikers I was out for the week. How was I going to explain to Coach?

When Mom rang the dinner bell, I didn't run downstairs like usual. I walked instead, wondering if she was still as mad as she'd been that morning.

To my surprise, she was her normal self, and I made it through the meal without causing any problems. I was thirsty, but I didn't drink more than anyone else. And when I finished my plate of spaghetti, I didn't ask for more. Instead, I stood up and cleared the table, even though it was Aiden's turn.

He seemed to think he was getting away with something, because he hurried back to his dungeon before anyone else noticed.

"I've got some homework to do," I said when I was finished.

Mom nodded, but didn't say anything, so I left her and my sisters and headed upstairs.

* * *

When Dad got home from his shift a couple of hours later, I heard Kate and Zoe race to the door to greet him. I didn't feel like going down there, so I stayed where I was.

The sounds of Mom reheating his dinner and their muffled voices floated up to me, but I couldn't hear what they were actually saying.

About ten minutes later, there was a knock on my door.

"Come in," I called.

When the door opened, I watched both of my parents walk in. I looked at their serious expressions and felt my stomach sink. Had they decided to make my punishment last two weeks instead of one? Or worse?

I had to do something. Fast.

"I've been thinking about what I did," I told them before they could speak.

"And?" Mom asked quietly.

I took a deep breath.

I looked her right in the eye and said, "I'm really sorry."

"And why are you sorry?"

"Throwing away the sheets was a stupid thing to do."

"Yes, it was," Mom said. She glanced at Dad, who nodded for her to go ahead. "We've been thinking about it, too, and perhaps the punishment I gave you is a bit . . . harsh."

I blinked hard, thinking I must have heard her wrong.

"Harsh?"

"Actually, Zoe gave me an earful after dinner," Mom said. "The word she used was 'mean.'"

"I didn't ask her to do that, Mom. She was—"

"Being Zoe?" she asked, starting to smile.

"Look, Sam," Dad said, "we know how much you love soccer."

"I do!"

"And we don't want you to let your team down."

"Me, neither," I agreed.

"We also don't want to jeopardize your chance to be captain."

I didn't know what jeopardize meant, but I felt tingles up and down my arms.

Were they actually changing their minds?

"Now, I think you realize what you did was wrong," Mom said.

They were!

"I do! I totally do."

Dad looked at her, then back at me. "We've decided that dishes and garbage duty for two weeks is a more suitable punishment."

My heart started to race. "So, I won't miss any soccer?"

"No," they both answered at once.

"Not even the practices?" I asked, grinning. "Are you serious?"

"Yes," Dad said.

I couldn't believe how lucky I was! I'd been so sure the white C was out of reach. It had never crossed my mind that things could turn around. And they had.

"You're really serious?" I asked again.

When they nodded, I ran over to hug them both.

My dream was still alive!

"Thank you, thank you, thank you." My voice was muffled by Mom's sweater.

"I never thought I'd see you this excited about dishes," Mom murmured against the top of my head.

* * *

It may not sound like much of an accomplishment, but I didn't wet the bed again. I never thought something like that would fall into gold-star territory, but each time I woke up to dry pajamas and sheets, I congratulated myself.

My solution was simple, too. All I had to do was stick to my plan and not drink after dinner. A dry bed was worth the terrible thirst.

Chapter
SEVEN

My next few practices were excellent, probably because I knew how close I'd come to missing out. I worked as hard as I could, and it wasn't just for Coach or the hope of being team captain. It was because I was so happy to be there, tearing up the turf with some of my closest friends.

"I'm *back*," I told Emily in the car after the second practice.

She smiled at me and said, "You were never gone, you goof," even though she knew I'd meant I had my moves back.

"Nice hustle out there," Dad said. "I saw you score during the scrimmage."

"Twice," I told him, glad he'd noticed. "And Emily did, too."

"Just once," she said, shrugging.

"It only takes one goal to win," Dad said.

We dropped Emily off at her house, and when Dad parked in our driveway, I was glad to be home. That is, until I walked into the kitchen and saw the stack of dirty plates, bowls and glasses in the sink.

I pulled off my sweatshirt, took a deep breath and stepped toward the tower.

The closer I got, the worse it looked. There were glasses coated with a film of dried chocolate milk, piled on top of bowls with baked-on macaroni and cheese.

Kate and Zoe.

* * *

On Saturday morning, Mom, Zoe, Kate and I had a big breakfast of French toast and strawberries. Then we gathered our things and drove forty minutes to my game.

I climbed out of the car and walked across the wet grass, which was scattered with orange and red leaves. More fell from the trees around me, flashing bits of color on the way down.

I joined the rest of the Strikers on the field. Most of the girls were passing balls back and forth while a couple took shots on goal.

Once both teams had warmed up, the ref blew her whistle and the game was on.

I played harder than ever before, and knowing how close I'd come to missing the game made me appreciate it even more.

Just before halftime, we were ahead by one goal, and I was already daydreaming about a win.

Emily passed me the ball. It went kind of high, so I headed it to the ground, glad for all the hours Aiden had spent throwing balls at my forehead for practice.

I got control of the ball with my feet, and I checked to see who stood between me and the goal.

Dribbling forward, I dodged around their right half, barely hearing the sound of the crowd cheering me on.

I was closing in on my target, and the goalie was looking a little nervous. She was crouched, hands in front, moving from one foot to the other every time I tapped the ball.

"Go for it, Sam!" Emily shouted from behind me.

"Take your time!" Coach Donaldson shouted even louder.

I always listened to what Coach said, so I took a breath and checked my options.

The goalie wasn't tall, but she had a pretty good reach. I was going to have to shoot fairly high to get it above her gloved fingertips.

I took my time, dribbling closer. When it felt just right, I kicked the ball, high and hard.

Just like I'd hoped, it soared right over her hands.

Yes!

My teammates screamed and shouted, pulling me into a hug just as the ref blew her whistle to end the half.

Then, a weird, light-headed feeling came over me, and I had to close my eyes for a few seconds to get my balance again.

I was actually *dizzy* with happiness.

Or so I thought.

* * *

The second half was about to start, but I was so thirsty and tired. I gulped some more orange Gatorade, hoping that would help.

"Are you okay?" Emily asked.

I nodded. "Yeah. I'm good."

Five minutes in, I noticed that things were getting kind of . . . blurry. I rubbed my eyes, but that didn't help at all. I felt awful.

What the heck was going on?

When the ref blew her whistle against a penalty, I was actually relieved that I could stop running for a few seconds. I rested my hands on my knees and closed my eyes, hoping that when I opened them, everything would be normal again.

I tried to take a slow, deep breath, but my heart was racing.

The ref blew her whistle again. I knew I had to get back in the game, but I felt really tired. Like, too tired to move.

I waited a second or two, trying to catch my breath.

"Samantha?" Mom shouted from the sidelines.

I lifted a hand to let her know I was okay, even though I wasn't.

"Samantha!" she shouted again, and this time her voice was closer. I could hear her breathing hard and knew she was running across the field toward me.

I stared at my feet, trying to focus, but my cleats, the grass and everything else looked blurry, no matter how hard I blinked.

The ref blew her whistle again.

"Samantha!" Mom was next to me, pulling me against her body, and it felt really good to lean against her.

"What's wrong?" she asked.

"I don't know," I admitted, starting to feel scared. "I'm so tired and everything looks blurry. I can't catch my breath."

"You feel hot," Mom said.

"Is everything okay?" Coach asked, coming from the sidelines as Mom walked me off the field.

"I don't think so," Mom said softly.

All of the other parents were staring at us, looking

worried. Kate and Zoe came running over, with a million questions.

"Sam?" Emily called.

"I'm going to take her to the doctor," Mom said, loud enough for everyone to hear. "Kate, Zoe, get in the car."

Emily's mom was there. "Beth, why don't I take Kate and Zoe home with me?" She bent down and put her arms on my sisters' shoulders.

"Thanks, Heather. That would be great. I'll call Jason and get him to pick them up in a bit," Mom said.

One of the dads had lifted me up and was carrying me to the car. He told me I was going to be fine.

I hoped he was right.

* * *

Of course, it was Saturday, and when we were halfway to Dr. Sharma's office, Mom realized it would be closed.

"There's a clinic on Oak Street," she muttered as she turned the car around, running up on the curb as she did it. She seemed worried.

We lurched into the opposite lane, and when the car bumped back down onto the road, I thought for sure I'd throw up.

"Just a couple of minutes and we'll be there, Sam," Mom said.

I was too afraid to open my mouth to answer her.

We made it to Oak Street, but we passed one block after another with no sign of a clinic.

"I was sure it was down here," Mom said, then glanced at me. I must have looked as bad as I felt, because she immediately said, "Forget it. We're going to Emergency."

* * *

"In here, please," the nurse said. She got me to sit on a bed in a small, curtained-off room. As she took my temperature and checked my blood pressure, she asked me a few questions. Then she tested my blood.

She told us that my blood sugars were really high, whatever that meant. Then she left us to wait for the doctor.

Mom called Dad to tell him where we were and about the blood sugar thing. Most of her side of the conversation was "I don't know" and "we're still waiting."

Dad wanted to talk to me, so she put me on the phone for a quick hello, but I didn't feel like saying much.

Soon the curtain was pushed aside by a doctor with white hair and a nurse with curly blond hair.

"Hello," the doctor said, reaching to shake Mom's hand. "I'm Dr. Vincent and this is Nurse Benson."

"Tamara," the nurse said, smiling.

We introduced ourselves, and then we waited while Dr. Vincent flipped through some pages on his clipboard.

"You've had a bit of a scare today," he finally said.

I nodded, then asked, "What's wrong with me?"

"That's what we've been figuring out. We've got some questions for you, Sam."

I glanced at Mom, who gave me an encouraging smile.

"Okay," I told him.

"Have you been feeling unusual lately?"

What kind of a question was that?

"Unusual?" I asked.

"Have you been unusually thirsty?"

How did he know that?

"I guess so."

He nodded and wrote something down. "So, you're making a lot of visits to the bathroom?"

I blushed, but nodded. If he knew about being thirsty and peeing all the time, would he know about wetting the bed, too?

I sure hoped not.

"What about sweetness of the breath?" Tamara asked.

What? Were these people crazy?

I started to shake my head, then remembered Kate saying I smelled like candy. "Maybe," I said softly.

Three out of three, so far.

What was I going to be a match for?

"Weight loss?" Tamara asked.

I nodded, thinking of the size-eight leggings.

"Any problems at night?" Dr. Vincent asked.

Great.

"Um . . ." I looked at Mom and bit my lip.

"If there's something the doctor should know, it's important to tell him," she said.

I took a deep breath. "I . . . uh . . . wet the bed." I stared at my hands in my lap, too embarrassed to look anyone in the eye.

I heard Mom gasp, but Dr. Vincent spoke before she could say anything. "How many times?" he asked.

"Twice," I said, waiting for Mom to ask me why I hadn't told her or get mad at me for keeping it a secret.

"The sheets," she whispered, then nodded like she understood. She didn't say anything else, but she put her hand on my shoulder to give it a squeeze. I was so relieved, I felt tears sting my eyes.

"That's normal," Dr. Vincent said.

Shocked, I jerked my head up and stared at him. "I'm *twelve*," I told him. "That's not normal at all."

"I meant for someone with your condition," he said.

"My condition?" I asked, feeling a little ball of dread growing inside my stomach.

"You have very high blood sugar," he said.

I noticed that Dr. Vincent and Tamara suddenly looked serious.

I wished one of them would smile, so I didn't feel like something terrible was happening.

Or *was* something terrible happening?

Dr. Vincent looked into my eyes. "They called us down here because we're part of the hospital's diabetes team."

"Oh," I said, barely breathing.

"Your blood sugar is very high right now, which leads us to believe you have diabetes."

Mom gasped, then rested a hand on my shoulder. When I looked at her, she tried really hard to smile, but she looked shaken up.

I turned back to the doctor.

"Okay . . ." I said. The word came out slowly and sounded more like a question than anything else.

Diabetes.

"Do you know what that is?" Tamara asked, looking concerned.

I nodded, thinking about Mr. Donovan down the street. He'd had to give up Tootsie Pops when he found out he had diabetes.

"It means I can't eat candy." I sighed as the words sunk in. Something terrible was definitely happening. No candy! How did I manage to get diabetes so close to Halloween?

"Well," Dr. Vincent said, "there are actually two different types." He cleared his throat. "The one you're probably thinking of is type 2. It's controlled mainly by diet and exercise."

The look on Mom's face made the ball of dread in my stomach grow a bit bigger.

"I don't have that kind?" I asked.

"No, you have type 1."

"Which is worse," I said quietly. I didn't know that for a fact, but I had a gut feeling.

"Well . . . it's generally more serious," the doctor said.

"*Worse*," I said again.

He looked at me for a few seconds, his head tilted to one side, like he was trying to make a decision. Then he said, "Your condition is serious, but we can control it."

"So," I asked, trying to act like I wasn't scared, "what's more serious than not being able to eat candy?"

He glanced at Mom, who told me, "You'll need to have insulin shots."

Insulin?

What the heck was insulin?

Wait! Did she say shots? Like more than one?

I took a shaky breath.

Okay, shots might not be too bad. I could handle the quick jab of a needle or two, then go home and be done with it.

"Now?" I asked, looking from Mom to Dr. Vincent to Tamara.

"Now and every day," the doctor said.

"Every day?" I gasped. "For how long?"

I waited for one of them to say it would be three days straight, a week or even two weeks.

"Forever," Mom said softly.

"What?" I choked. *"Forever?"*

"We're going to give you some insulin now," Dr. Vincent said. "And I'll explain things."

As Tamara gave me the needle, Mom let me squeeze her fingers as tight as I could. The shot took longer than a regular one because she had to make sure all of the insulin was inside of me.

I couldn't watch, so I looked into Mom's eyes while we counted to ten in a whisper.

"One Mississippi, two Mississippi . . ."

When we were done, Dr. Vincent began to talk, for what felt like hours, about all the things my body was and wasn't doing.

The basic idea is that everybody has an organ called a pancreas, and it's supposed to make something called insulin, which turns sugar and starches and other food into energy. But my stupid pancreas doesn't work. It's defective, like the ball pump Dad had to take back to Sportsville.

Only, I can't just go get a replacement. Or a refund.

"So," Dr. Vincent continued, like my head wasn't spinning, "because your pancreas doesn't produce insulin, your blood sugar level is affected. It can get too high, like it did today, and you may feel confused, tired, and nauseous. You might get a bit shaky, sweaty or weak and your vision can get blurry."

I nodded slowly as his words sank in. "So, I guess I'll have to make sure I keep my blood sugar levels really low."

Dr. Vincent shook his head. "I'm afraid it's not that simple. Once you're taking insulin, low blood sugar comes with its own set of problems. You could lose consciousness, possibly have a seizure, or—"

"Please stop," I said, interrupting him.

"I'm sorry?" Dr. Vincent asked.

"Please stop telling me all of this bad stuff," I begged. "I don't want to hear any more."

"Honey," Mom whispered, "I know it's hard, but we have to learn about this."

"The good part, Samantha," Tamara said, "is that we know what's wrong, and we know how to manage this disease."

"With shots," I said, my voice breaking. Every day, for the rest of my life.

"Yes, shots are one piece," Dr. Vincent agreed. "But there are actually three things we use: medication, diet and exercise. When those three things work together, your blood sugar levels should stay within the right range. And you don't even have to give up candy."

Then I found out that I'd need three or four shots a day, and I'd have to test my blood before each meal *and* at bedtime. I was supposed to prick my fingertip with a needle and touch the blood to a test strip, which I'd then put into a little machine. The machine would show me my blood sugar level, which was supposed to be within a target range.

Dr. Vincent said that if I didn't take the right amount of insulin, I could get really sick from that, too.

The whole thing was already complicated, and I groaned when he started talking about carbohydrates and all kinds of junk I didn't have the energy to try to understand.

All I wanted in the world was to put on my coziest PJs and climb into my own bed with Tony purring next to me. I wanted a hug from my dad and a cuddle with Zoe and Kate. I wanted everything to be normal, even if normal was Aiden ignoring me in public or green beans on my plate at dinnertime.

I couldn't wait to get home.

But it turned out I'd have to.

Tamara tested my blood sugar again and showed the number to Dr. Vincent.

"Can we go now?" I asked.

"I'm sorry, Samantha," Dr. Vincent said. "We need to get your blood sugar down first. We're going to keep you here at the hospital overnight."

"What for?" I asked.

"I'm going to observe you, and Tamara will give you and your parents some training on how to manage the diabetes. They'll learn how to inject insulin and—"

What?

"My *parents* are going to give me the shots?" I gasped. Mom and Dad weren't doctors.

Tamara nodded. "Yes, your parents and, eventually, you."

I swallowed hard.

Forget wanting to go home and see my family before snuggling up in bed. What I really needed to do was travel back in time. I needed to start the day all over again. And this time, get it right.

But I couldn't do that, either.

When Dr. Vincent and Tamara finally left the room, Mom and I didn't say anything right away. She pulled me into a tight hug, and I could smell our laundry detergent and her perfume. I could feel her breath on my neck and her heartbeat against my chest. Both were slow and steady, which helped make mine slow and steady, too.

I was exhausted, upset and totally confused by what had happened and why it was happening to me. Just a few hours earlier, I'd been the happiest girl on the Strikers. And now?

The worst part was that I'd been too afraid to ask Dr. Vincent the one question I'd really wanted to. More than what I could eat or how many shots I needed, I wanted to know if I was still going to be able to play soccer.

"I wish I was out on the field," I whispered.

Mom's arms tightened around me. "If wishes were nickels, we'd all be rich."

"If wishes were fishes, we'd eat them with chips," I answered like I always did, but my voice was barely more than a whisper.

"If wishes were kisses, I'd have chapped lips," she said, pressing hers against the top of my head.

* * *

After another insulin shot, they moved me to a room upstairs. Mom stayed with me for the whole afternoon until she traded places with Dad before dinner.

A new nurse came in and did another test. I'd learned

that my good range for blood sugar was between seventy and one hundred and eighty. The test came in at two hundred and forty-seven, so I needed another shot.

"I'm sorry I wasn't here earlier, Triple S," Dad said when the nurse had left us alone. "I picked up Zoe and Kate from Emily's house—"

"Did we win?" I asked.

He smiled. "I should have known that would be your first question."

"Did we?"

"Yes. Five to two." He cleared his throat. "So, the doctor says—"

"Did Emily tell you who scored the last goal?" I asked, desperate to be distracted.

"Zoe told me, actually. It was Kylie."

"Oh," I said, wishing it had been someone other than the highest scorer on the team.

I thought of everyone celebrating a win without me, and I wondered if it would be just the first time that happened.

* * *

Mom brought Kate and Zoe in later that evening, each carrying a little bouquet of flowers. I figured Aiden was with them, dragging his feet down the hallway to look cool or something.

But he wasn't.

"Are you okay?" Zoe asked.

I nodded. "Yeah."

"I was scared."

"I know," I said, trying to smile. "Sorry about that, Z."

"Were you tired?"

I cleared my throat. "Very tired."

"Did you—"

"Ask me to spell happiness," Kate interrupted, climbing up to sit on the side of my bed.

"Does the bed go up and down?" Zoe asked.

"Yes," I told her, handing her the remote control and showing her which button to push. I should have known that was a mistake. In less than a minute I was feeling seasick from all of the ups and downs, and my face must have been green.

"That's enough," Dad told her.

Zoe sighed and handed the remote back to me.

"Seriously, Samantha," Kate said. "Ask me to spell happiness."

"I'm kind of tired."

"So? I'm the one doing the spelling."

"Dad?" I said, and he got them both to quiet down.

"Aren't you happy to see us?" Zoe asked.

"Of course, I am. I missed you guys."

"A lot?" Zoe asked.

"Yes."

"More than you missed Aiden?" Kate asked.

"Where is he?"

"He couldn't make it," Mom said quietly.

"Why not?"

"He had some other things he needed to do."

"But—"

"He sends his love."

I frowned. "Did he actually say that?"

"Not in so many words," Mom said, "but we all know it's the truth."

I didn't know what "other things" my brother needed to do, but if *he'd* been in the hospital, I would have begged to visit him.

* * *

While I was in the hospital, my diagnosis and the changes it would mean for me slowly started to sink in.

And, after a bunch of training and more talk about sugar levels, carbs, test strips and insulin than I could ever hope to remember, I never wanted to hear the word diabetes again.

But I knew that was impossible, because I'd also learned the best I could do with diabetes was manage it, control it and live with it.

Because there was no cure.

Chapter
EIGHT

When Dr. Vincent told me I could go home, I was so happy, I could have eaten a whole plate of green beans without even flinching. At the same time, I was working up the nerve to ask him the most important question of all, though I was terrified of what he might say.

"So," I finally said, once I was dressed in my own clothes and ready to leave. "I was just wondering . . ."

"Yes?"

"Can I play soccer?" My voice cracked on the last word.

He shook his head. "Not yet, Samantha."

My heart sunk. "When?" I asked, afraid that he was going to say never. What would I do then?

"We'll have to see how things go," he said, giving me a pat on the back.

I almost started crying, but I bit my bottom lip and held it in. I glanced over at Mom, who tried to smile.

"I'm going to refer you to a diabetes center near your home. Dr. Elliott is a friend of mine who works there." He waited until I made eye contact. "She'll talk to you about playing soccer."

I tried to imagine my life without practices and games to look forward to. I thought about my teammates, and how much I loved hanging out with them.

I tried to picture myself stuck on the sidelines, no longer part of the team.

And I couldn't.

Soccer was my life.

Soccer *was* my life.

Now diabetes *is* my life.

* * *

While Mom loaded my stuff into the car, I just stood to the side, trying not to cry. But by the time we'd climbed in and buckled our seat belts, she knew something was up.

"What's wrong?" she asked, her forehead wrinkling with worry.

"He said I can't play soccer." I felt tears in my eyes.

"Shh," Mom whispered, wrapping an arm around me.

"I'm not going to be a Striker anymore."

"Samantha," Mom said, pulling me closer. "You're getting wound up about nothing."

"Nothing?" I choked, shocked. "It's—"

"I don't mean *soccer*," she interrupted. "I'm talking about Dr. Vincent's comment. I was standing right next to you, and all he said was that we'd have to see how things went. We'll go to this diabetes center and—"

"But if they—"

"We'll figure it out then. In the meantime, it won't do any good to expect the worst."

But the worst was all I seemed to be getting lately! "What if—"

Mom took my face in her hands. "Where is the incredibly determined girl I know?"

"Here," I said quietly.

"That girl wouldn't let the thought of life without soccer enter her head until she had no other choice."

"I know, but—"

"We have no idea what's going to happen tomorrow, let alone a week from now, so why not think positive thoughts?" She kissed my forehead and I felt my shoulders relax.

"Can we go home now?" I asked.

"We have to do a little shopping on the way," she told me, pulling out of the parking spot. "Tamara gave me the address of a store that specializes in diabetes supplies."

Not exactly what I felt like shopping for.

Of course, I didn't feel like shopping at all. I just wanted to be home. I couldn't wait to walk in the front door, greeted by the familiar smell of banana bread and lemon dish detergent. And the only thing I wanted to do was flop on the couch with my favorite blanket, my sisters cuddled next to me.

Mom and I didn't say too much on the way to the store, and that was okay with me. I had plenty to think about.

When we got there, she pulled out a list of things I needed. We started at the top with an insulin pen, which looked like a regular pen, but fatter.

With a needle instead of a ballpoint.

"Those come in six different colors," the lady behind the counter said when Mom found the type we were looking for.

"You choose, honey," Mom said.

I looked them over and picked a sparkly green one, almost the exact same color as my Strikers uniform.

I held onto the pen, wondering what made Tamara think I'd ever be able to give myself insulin shots.

Next we looked for the blood sugar tester and test strips. Tamara had recommended a particular brand, so that made it easy. The tester was pretty small and looked like the pedometer Dad wore to count his steps, so that wasn't too bad.

We slowly worked our way down the list until we had a full basket. The last item we needed was a medical ID bracelet.

There was a big display case at the front of the store filled with shiny silver ones. I took a look and saw that all of the bracelets had the medical alert snake logo (which I didn't like) stamped on them.

"On the back, we'll engrave *Type 1 Diabetes*," the lady said, like that was something I should be excited about.

So, I wouldn't just have diabetes inside me, I'd be *wearing* it, too.

"Can I see that one?" Mom asked, and the lady opened the back of the case to pull out a bracelet.

I didn't even look at it, because I'd seen what I wanted. It was green rubber, like the ones our school baseball team had sold as part of a fundraiser last year.

"I like that one," I said, pointing to it.

Barely looking at it, Mom said, "No. We'll get a silver one."

"They're actually stainless steel," the lady said.

"Even better."

"Wait, why can't I have that one?" I asked.

Mom sighed. "Because it doesn't look like a medical ID bracelet."

"I know," I told her. "That's the whole point. It's way cooler."

Mom didn't look convinced. "People won't know you're diabetic."

"We *do* stamp the information on the bracelets in a different color," the lady said.

"Do you have yellow?" I asked, thinking of my uniform.

"We do."

I looked at Mom. "Please?" I begged.

We compromised by getting one of each bracelet.

* * *

Back in the car, I tried not to think about the end of my soccer career. Instead, I counted off the things I was looking forward to at home.

I'd only been gone a night, but I couldn't wait to taste Mom's cooking. Of course, I wouldn't be able to eat the same as I used to, and she'd have to do the crazy carb calculations for every dish, but it would be nice to leave the boring hospital food behind.

It would be nice to get back to normal.

But when I finally walked through the front door, it wasn't normal at all.

Everything looked the same as ever, but it *felt* totally different. Dad gave me a big hug, like he hadn't seen me for weeks. Aiden, Kate and Zoe stood in the kitchen doorway, all stiff and weird. Aiden nodded at me while the girls just stared, like I was an alien or something.

"I don't get a hug?" I asked them.

My sisters nodded and walked over to give me the weakest hugs in history.

"I'm not going to break," I told them when they let go. "You guys were all over me at the hospital."

"I know," Kate said, but she still looked kind of scared.

"And I'm not contagious."

"Uh-huh," Zoe said, backing away.

I was disappointed, but tried not to show it. I'd been looking forward to coming home for days, and now it felt . . . wrong.

Aiden slipped out of the room without saying anything.

"Teenagers, huh?" Mom said in a voice that was way too cheerful.

"Yeah," I sighed. "Teenagers."

Dad went outside to unload the car while Mom, the girls and I all stood in the hallway. It was awkward, like I was a guest and they were supposed to entertain me.

"Do you want some water, Samantha?" Mom asked.

"No, thanks." And if I did, I could get it myself.

I turned and saw that Kate was still staring at me, like I was going to explode into a million pieces.

And that's when I kind of did.

All I'd wanted was to walk into my own house and

feel *normal*. I wanted to eat what I felt like and sleep for a whole night without being woken up for tests. I didn't want to have needles all the time or carry a kit everywhere, and I didn't want to wear jewelry that advertised the stupid disease.

I hated diabetes.

I wanted my old life back.

"Aren't you going offer to spell something?" I snapped at Kate.

"What?" she asked, blinking hard.

"Spell something."

"Uh . . . I don't know what to—"

"How about *hospital*?" I suggested.

She shook her head, "I don't—"

"What about *emergency*?" Little bits of spit sprayed out of my mouth when I said it.

"Samantha," Mom warned.

"What? How about *diabetes*, Kate?" I practically shouted. "Or maybe *insulin*?"

"Stop it," Kate whispered.

"Why don't you try to spell *miserable, messed-up life*?"

"What's going on in here?" Dad asked from the front door.

"Samantha's just—" Mom said, but I cut her off.

"*Mad*, Dad. I'm mad, and I want to scream as loud as I can, okay?"

Dad looked at Mom, who put her hands on her hips.

"Now is not the time for hysterics," she said.

"Really?" I snapped. "It seems like the perfect time for it. My whole life is—"

"Enough!" Dad shouted.

Dad *never* shouted, so I froze with surprise.

Kate's and Zoe's eyes were huge.

"That's enough," Dad said more quietly. "Samantha, go to the kitchen. And you two," he said, pointing at my sisters, "go play upstairs."

They turned and ran.

I followed Mom and Dad into the kitchen and slumped on a stool, my arms folded on the countertop.

"Look," Dad said, "we know this has been tough and—"

"It's not—"

"I'm not finished," he said firmly. "Your diagnosis and everything that comes with it is a lot to swallow. Mom and I know that."

"I—"

"All anger will do is make it harder, Samantha," Dad went on. "You've got to turn that emotion into something else. Something positive."

Something positive?

How could a disease with no cure ever be something positive?

I shook my head. "I can't."

"You're going to have to," Mom said. "And we're all here to love and support you."

"We're all in this together," Dad added.

"That's the thing, though. We aren't. I'm the only one who has to live with this. I'm the one getting shots and . . ." I sighed. "I'm just . . ." I tried to think of a word that summed up everything I was feeling. I imagined never running onto the field again. And I thought about how rotten I'd felt on the field the day before. I swallowed hard. "Scared."

"Of course you're scared," Mom said, reaching over to rub my back in slow, steady circles.

"You have every right to be," Dad added. "You're just a kid, and this is a huge thing you're dealing with." He looked at Mom, then back at me. "You want to know the truth, Triple S?"

"What?"

"We're all scared," Dad said.

That wasn't what I wanted to hear.

"But we're going to help you in every way we can."

"We all love you," Mom said, still rubbing my back.

Suddenly, I was totally exhausted. I didn't want to talk anymore, or think, or . . . anything.

But Dad wasn't finished.

"This diabetes thing is new to all of us, so it's going to take some time to get up to speed on all of the things we need to know."

"And I'm sure you'll be frustrated from time to time," Mom said. "And we understand that." She tucked some stray hairs behind my ear. "But that doesn't mean you get to take out your frustration on the people who love you and are trying to help you."

"I'm sorry," I said softly. "I didn't mean to—"

"We know," Mom said, pulling me into a hug.

"I'm going to lie down for a while," I told them when she let go.

I started toward the stairs, but Dad said, "Wait, Samantha."

"What?"

"Mom and I want you to sleep down here for now."

"But I—"

"We'd like you down here," he repeated. "Close to our room."

"But where?" I asked, feeling my heart sink. All I wanted was my own bed. Tony curled next to me, googly-eyed Clyde propped by my feet.

All I wanted was *normal*.

"In the office," Dad said. "I moved one of the camping cots in there and—"

"A camping cot? Why can't I just sleep in my room?"

"Because we'd feel better if you were down here. It's just for a night or two."

"Two nights?" I looked toward the stairs.

"Just until we get you settled in," Mom said.

I sighed. "How am I supposed to feel settled if I'm not even in my own bed?"

Mom ignored the question. "Dad brought your blanket and pillow down and got everything set up for you. Just go have a little nap and no one will bother you."

They left me in the kitchen, and I realized that it was the first time I'd been alone in a while. I didn't feel like having a nap. I didn't feel like doing *anything*.

I was about to get myself a glass of juice when I remembered I couldn't. It was different in the hospital, when other people were deciding what I could eat and drink and I didn't have to think about it. At home it was going to be a lot trickier. I couldn't pour myself an OJ without testing my stupid blood first.

Instead of getting something to drink, I wandered into the TV room. Aiden was in the big recliner, watching a movie.

"Hey," he said, only looking at me for a second.

"Hey." I pulled my favorite blanket from the pile on the rocking chair and sat on the couch.

"Have you seen this?" Aiden asked, staring at the screen.

"Yeah."

I waited for him to say something about the hospital or ask me about the diabetes, but he didn't say *anything*.

He knew I'd been in the hospital and been diagnosed with a disease that would never go away, and all he could ask about was whether I'd seen some dumb movie?

Didn't he even care?

Suddenly, I didn't feel like watching TV anymore.

I folded up my blanket, and as I left the room, Aiden mumbled, "See ya."

I ended up falling asleep on the office cot until dinnertime.

When Mom woke me up, I was groggy and felt like I could have slept for another couple of hours.

She pulled out my diabetes kit and said, "Let's see how things are."

Mom stuck a test strip into the tester, and I held up my pinkie finger for her. The rest of my fingertips were sore from pokes at the hospital. She held the small testing pen against my skin, and when she clicked the button, a needle shot out, lightning fast. I squeezed my fingertip until there was a big enough drop of blood to test. Then I touched it to the strip, and we both watched the screen flash.

I sighed when I saw my blood sugar number: two

hundred and ten.

I needed insulin.

"Come on," Mom said, leading me into the kitchen. She rang the dinner bell, and my brother and sisters came running.

"What's going on?" Aiden grumbled when he didn't see any food.

"We're ending the mystery right now," Mom said to everyone. "I'm going to give Samantha her insulin shot."

I was kind of embarrassed to have an audience, and I was a little nervous, too. It would be Mom's first time injecting me without a doctor standing right beside her.

I lifted up the bottom of my T-shirt and pinched the skin above my jeans.

Mom put my insulin dose into the green pen and held the pen against my stomach. I felt a sharp sting, and I looked into her eyes while we counted ten Mississippis together.

When we were finished, I saw that Kate and Zoe looked scared to death and Aiden wasn't looking at all.

I couldn't help feeling disappointed. Seeing what Mom had to do was supposed to make them more comfortable, not freak them out.

I had to wait a few minutes before I could eat, so Aiden, Kate, Zoe and I went to the TV room.

"Did it hurt?" Kate whispered when she sat down

next to me on the couch.

"It's not too bad," I told her. It was true. The actual shot wasn't nearly as bad as dreading it.

"Want me to kiss it better?" Zoe asked.

"How about a kiss right here?" I asked, pointing at my cheek.

She climbed up next to me and gave me a wet one. "Now you're all better."

I wished.

* * *

I had a hard time falling asleep that night, mostly because I knew Mom or Dad had to test me at midnight and again at four in the morning.

I woke up when Mom did it, but I fell right back to sleep and into a bunch of weird dreams the second she was finished.

When Dad tested me at four, I didn't even feel it. He must have been practicing on the heart-shaped cushion Tamara gave him during training.

I might not have remembered or understood everything I'd heard at the hospital, but I knew that if my number was high, I needed insulin. If it was too low, I needed some of the emergency candy in the pantry or some juice or a gross-tasting glucose tab.

Somehow I stayed level all night and didn't need anything. But when Mom tested me again at eight the next morning, my number was two hundred and twenty-six. Out came the green pen, and we counted another ten Mississippis as she injected me.

"I think an extra day at home is a good idea," Mom whispered, leaving me to fall back to sleep.

Chapter
NINE

Later that morning, I was starting to think I'd lose my mind from boredom when I had an idea.

Maybe I'd feel better if I got busy doing something normal, like making lunch. I headed to the fridge to see what kind of ingredients we had.

When I swung the door open, I stopped. Instead of the juice boxes and cheese sticks that were usually on the bottom shelf, all I saw were boxes and bottles.

I picked up a bottle and read the label.

Insulin.

Part of me wanted to smash it on the floor, but I knew I was going to need it if I ever wanted to eat again.

And I definitely wanted to eat again.

We had a carton of eggs, so I decided to make egg

salad sandwiches. I put the eggs on the counter, along with some green onions, dill and mayonnaise.

I was just checking for bread when I heard Mom behind me.

"What are you doing?" she gasped.

I spun around. "Nothing. Just making egg salad."

Her eyes were wide. "Samantha, you can't eat that without—"

"I wasn't going to eat it *now*," I told her. "I'm making it for lunch. For both of us."

"But I have a meal planned for lunch," she said, pointing at the new whiteboard on the wall. She'd written every single meal for the week on there.

"I know there's a plan and everything." I sighed. "It's just that egg salad sounded really good right now."

Mom nodded slowly. "Okay, Triple S, but we'll have to figure out the carbohydrates before we eat."

"I know," I told her.

"We'll look up the ingredients in that dietary guide I bought and—"

"Mom?" I interrupted.

"Yes?"

"Can we worry about that part later?"

Her shoulders relaxed and she tried to smile. "Sure," she nodded. "Sure, we can." Then she came over and started chopping onions.

That afternoon I was lying on the couch, watching an infomercial on TV and wishing I'd gone to school, when the doorbell rang.

"I'll get it," Mom said before I could get up.

When she opened the door, I heard Emily say, "Hi, Ms. Stevens. Is it okay for us to visit Sam?"

I was so happy to hear my best friend's voice, I almost started crying. Of course, a lot of things were making me emotional since my diagnosis, but this time it was a good thing.

Seeing Emily would make me feel *normal*.

"Absolutely," Mom said. "Come on in, girls."

I turned down the volume on the TV and looked up as Emily, Mai and Sara all came around the corner. They must have come straight from school, since they had their bags and backpacks with them. I wished I'd spent my afternoon at Evergreen Middle School.

"Hey, Samantha!" Emily said, smiling really wide.

"Hi," I said.

Mai gave me a little wave while Sara smiled awkwardly at me then quickly looked away.

"How are you doing?" Emily asked.

That was a pretty tricky question. I wasn't sure I had the words to describe how I'd been feeling for the past few days. Up and down and all over the place.

"Fine," I said, because it seemed like the easiest answer.

"Cool," Sara said. She and Mai looked toward the TV screen.

I waited for someone to say something. *Anything*.

"Kylie was going to come," Sara finally said, "but she . . . couldn't."

One look at Emily's expression told me that wasn't entirely true.

"I think she was just . . . *uncomfortable*," Mai said.

"Uncomfortable?" I asked, surprised.

"*Everybody* misses you at school," Emily quickly added, before I could ask what Mai meant.

"So, what did I miss?" I asked. "Sara?"

"Nothing much," she said with a shrug. "It's the same old thing, you know?"

They all nodded.

"How was the rest of the game Saturday?"

"Good," Mai said.

They all nodded again.

"My dad said we won." I moved over to make room for them on the couch.

"Yeah, we did." Emily perched on the edge of a cushion, but no one else sat down.

The room was silent.

"So," Sara eventually said, looking anywhere but at me.

"So," Mai repeated, but didn't add anything.

Why were they acting so weird?

Emily cleared her throat. "I tried to come and see you in the hospital, but they said it was family only."

I nodded. "Mom told me. Thanks for trying."

"Kylie heard you were in a coma," Sara said, finally making eye contact again.

"What? No. I was feeling kind of sick and stuff, but I wasn't *unconscious*. I was awake the whole time."

"Oh," she said. "Cool."

"Um, is that going to happen again?" Mai asked. "You know, your mom having to carry you off the field?"

"She didn't carry me—"

"Brianne's dad did," Sara interrupted.

"Yeah . . . but not off the field. Just to the car."

"That's what I meant," Mai said. "Is that going to happen again?"

How was I supposed to know? "I hope not."

She winced. "But you don't know for sure?"

"Uh . . . no."

Emily bit her lip, then said, "It was scary."

"Yeah," Sara said. "Everybody freaked out."

It seemed like they were *still* freaking out. Everyone but Emily, anyway. I was starting to wish she had come over by herself.

"Would anyone like a drink?" Mom asked from the doorway. "I have orange juice, lemonade, milk or water."

"No, thank you," they all seemed to say at once.

"We should probably go," Sara said.

She glanced at Mai, who quickly said, "Yeah."

"But you just got here," Mom said. Apparently she didn't notice how awkward everyone was.

"We just wanted to make sure Sam was okay," Mai explained as she and Sara started walking toward the door.

But I *wasn't* okay! Not even slightly. Sure, I'd said I was fine, but couldn't my teammates tell that I wasn't? Didn't they understand that I was a hundred times more freaked out about the diabetes than they were?

"Are you coming, Em?" Sara asked.

"No, I'm going to hang out here for a while."

"Okay. Good seeing you, Sam," Mai called out as Sara waved.

But they hadn't really seen me at all.

"I'll leave you two alone," Mom said, disappearing into the kitchen.

Emily and I were silent for a moment or two.

"Well, that was . . . totally weird," she said.

To my surprise, we both burst out laughing. It felt really, really good.

"So," I said, once we'd calmed down. "Are they scared of me now?"

Emily could tell I was serious. "Not scared of *you*, Sam. Scared of the situation."

"The diabetes."

"Well, yeah. They don't understand it."

"Hey, I don't totally understand it either, but I'm figuring it out. You know, they could have asked me whatever they wanted to."

She frowned. "I shouldn't have brought them."

"You didn't know they were going to be like that."

Mom brought in a couple of glasses of ice water and set them on the coffee table.

"Thanks, Ms. Stevens," Emily said.

"Thank *you*," Mom answered, giving her shoulder a squeeze before she left us alone again.

"I missed social studies today. I guess we're behind on our project," I said.

"Ms. Handel said she'd give us an extension if we need it."

"Cool."

"So," Emily said, looking a bit nervous. "Before you got sick on the field, did you know anything was wrong?"

I'd spent so much time talking to doctors, nurses and my family about what was happening to me, it didn't really bother me anymore. So, I took a deep breath and told her.

Everything.

I watched her eyes get wide when I talked about the bed wetting, and she shook her head when I mentioned the thirst, the weight loss and how tired I'd felt.

"But you never said anything."

I shrugged. "I didn't know it meant anything."

She bit her lip, then asked, "So, what *does* it mean?"

I explained to her about the shots, the carbohydrates and everything else I knew about managing my diabetes. The more I talked and the more she listened, the easier it was.

"Wow," she said when I was finished. "I can't even imagine."

I sighed. "I can barely imagine it myself, and I'm living it."

"It's . . . *serious*, Sam."

"Yeah," I said softly. "It is."

* * *

After dinner that night, Dad called a Stevens family meeting, which was a surprise. The last one we had was when my parents told us we were taking a family vacation to Disney World. But, of course, this didn't have anything to do with a vacation.

When everyone was sitting down in the living room,

looking more excited than they should have, Dad pulled out a DVD about diabetes.

"As we all know, Samantha is going through some big changes right now."

Mom added, "Dad and I have been learning all about Sam's diabetes, and this video is going to help you kids understand. We all need to support her."

"I have a call I need to make," Aiden said, getting up to go.

"What did your mother just say?" Dad asked, sounding annoyed.

My brother rolled his eyes. "Can't I just—"

Mom shot him a look. "No."

He groaned and fell back against the cushions as the movie started.

I'd already seen it, so instead of watching the screen, I peeked at my brother and sisters to see how they were reacting.

Zoe's eyes were wide, and Kate was chewing her thumbnail as she watched. Even though Aiden didn't want to be there, he never looked away from the video.

I was glad to see that they were all paying close attention, since it was pretty important stuff. Like, life-saving stuff.

When it ended, Mom asked whether anyone had questions.

"Is she going to be okay?" Kate asked.

Mom glanced at me, then back at Kate. "*Of course* she is. You saw the movie. She just has to be a little more careful than she used to."

A little? Yeah, right.

"Is she going to get all weird at soccer again?" Zoe asked.

Not if I never got to play again.

"A healthier diet and the insulin you saw Mom give her will help stop that from happening," Dad explained.

"Good," Kate said, looking relieved.

"But something serious could happen again," Mom said. "Which is why we have Big Red."

"Big *what*?" Aiden asked.

Dad set what looked like a small toolbox on the coffee table. I'd already seen it, so I knew there was a huge red needle inside. I also knew it contained something called glucagon, which could quickly raise my blood sugar level.

Dad explained, "If Sam's blood sugar gets too low, she could faint or have a seizure—"

"A seizure?" Aiden interrupted.

Dad nodded. "She'll need this shot of glucagon immediately, so someone will have to inject her."

"Someone like a *doctor*, you mean," Aiden said. "Right?"

"No, someone like us," Dad corrected.

"Geez," Aiden said, shaking his head. "Who's going to be in charge of *that*?"

"All of us," Dad said, shrugging. "If we notice the symptoms that she's low, we have to act. That might mean something as simple as getting Sam some juice or candy. But if the situation is more serious, like a seizure—"

"We're supposed to use that?" Aiden asked, pointing at Big Red.

Dad gave him a long look. "Yes. Your sister's life could be at risk."

"She could die?" Kate gasped.

"She could die?" Zoe echoed.

I didn't know what to say, and it didn't look like my parents did, either.

The room was totally silent. Finally, Dad said, "Yes."

I blinked hard.

I'd had days to get used to knowing that, but it still took my breath away to hear it.

Dad held up Big Red. "That's why this is so important."

He demonstrated how it worked, and I watched my brother's face turn almost as red as the needle.

"This is crazy," Aiden said, getting up to leave.

"This is *reality*," Mom said, reaching for his arm to

stop him. "And we all need to be aware of it."

I don't know how much Aiden listened to after that, but he definitely didn't say anything else.

Mom and Dad led us into the kitchen so my siblings could see where we kept Big Red, my medication, my needles and all the rest of my gear. No one said a word. They just stared at it all.

Mom opened the cupboard under the sink and pulled out a bright orange tub.

"H-A-Z-A—" Kate started to spell, but Aiden cut her off.

"Hazardous waste?" he practically choked.

"It's for Sam's needles," Mom explained. "We can't put them in a regular garbage can or the recycling box."

"So it's only hazardous for *us*," he said sarcastically.

"Aiden." Dad gave him a look.

"Does anyone have any questions?" Mom asked.

"Where did you move the cookie jar to?" Zoe asked.

Mom sighed. "In the cupboard over the fridge."

"I can't reach there," she whined.

"Then get help when you want one."

Zoe looked disappointed, like they'd told her she'd have to run a marathon if she wanted a cookie.

Like *she* was the one whose life had changed for the worse.

"Okay, then," Dad said, clapping his hands once.

"Let's put our new knowledge to the test!"

"How?" asked Aiden.

"We're going to do a drill."

"Like a fire drill?" Kate looked excited.

"Well, kind of," Dad said, leading us back to the living room. "We're going to practice for an emergency."

"A Sam emergency?" Zoe asked.

Dad nodded. "We're going to do a little practice run."

Zoe and Kate exchanged nervous looks.

"Triple S," Dad said. "You're going to—"

"I don't want to," I blurted.

Dad looked at me for a long moment then said, "Okay. Which of you two wants to play Sam?"

"I will," Kate said, raising her arm.

I sat on the couch, and Tony climbed into my lap right away. He started purring as soon as I rubbed his ears. Aiden sat on the other cushion but didn't even look at me.

"Okay," Dad said, directing Kate to the middle of the rug. He whispered into her ear, and she nodded a couple of times.

"Now," Dad said to the rest of us, "Kate's going to pretend to have a seizure. When she does, I want Aiden to spring into action. Ready?"

Kate, Zoe and Mom all said yes, but Aiden and I were silent.

"Go!" Dad said.

I expected Kate to drop to the ground right away, but she didn't. I couldn't take my eyes off her as she started to shake and swayed from one side to the other. She jerked her arms a bit and fell to the floor. Then she shook for a moment before lying totally still, like she was dead.

I tried to swallow the lump in my throat.

Was that what I would look like?

"Aiden!" Dad called. "I need you to react!"

I glanced at my brother, who looked as shocked as I was.

Instead of running to the kitchen to grab Big Red, he took off upstairs.

"Where are you going?" Dad yelled after him. "We're not finished!"

Mom must have seen how freaked out I was, because she pulled me into her arms and told Dad that was enough for one night.

The truth was, it was enough for a lifetime.

Chapter

TEN

The next day, I went back to school and Mom came in with me. I was really glad she did. Normally, I would have wanted to go in by myself, but with the diabetes, everything felt different and strange. As much as I hated to admit it, ever since I'd come home from the hospital, I wasn't as sure of anything as I used to be.

What I was most unsure about was how kids were going to act around me. After seeing Mai and Sara at my house, I worried that the rest of the kids would be awkward, too. Would they think I was contagious? Weird? Or just plain scary?

I wanted to feel like I was the same old Samantha, but I knew that wasn't me anymore.

The first bell had already rung, so the schoolyard

was empty. It was just me and Mom walking up the path toward the red brick building.

I took a deep breath, and when Mom reached for my hand, I let her hold it. I wouldn't have done that before, but now it made me feel safe.

When we got inside, I felt like I'd been gone for weeks or months instead of just a day.

That is, until I saw one of the cafeteria workers writing *Meatloaf* on the lunch board. Then it felt like I hadn't been gone at all.

My shoulders started to relax as we walked past the murals in the hall. They were so old that the kids who'd painted them were probably grandparents. I smiled when I saw the two cartoonish bluebirds that always reminded me of Kate and Zoe.

"Hey, Sam," Jamie Waters called out as he hurried into his homeroom class. "You're gonna be late!"

I waved back, happy that was all he'd said.

"Hi, Sam." Natalie Walker smiled as she walked by. "I hope you're feeling better."

"Thanks."

"Are you okay?" Mom whispered.

"Yes," I said. And, to my surprise, it was the truth.

I was breathing normally. My heart was steady.

I was going to be fine.

We met with the school nurse, Ms. Mitchell, in her

office. It was smaller than our bathroom, with just a cot, a little desk and a couple of cabinets inside. Her long, grey hair was pulled up in a bun on top of her head, and her dark brown eyes sparkled.

"So, you're going to take care of your own blood sugar tests, but you'll pay me a visit for your insulin shot as soon as the lunch bell rings, every day."

"Yes."

"And if your sugar is ever out of range or you're just plain not feeling well, you'll come here so I can help you, right?"

"Right."

"That sounds like a good plan." She smiled at me. "You've got some snacks with you in case you need something during class?"

"Yes."

"And, Mom," she said, turning to my mother. "You've got her set up with lunches that will keep her blood sugar level?"

"They should," she said.

Ms. Mitchell gave her a kind look. "It's like a second job sometimes."

I hadn't thought about that. Mom was the one who'd done all of the reading, studying and menu planning. I thought of the whiteboard menu in our kitchen. It *was* a lot of work.

"We're doing fine," Mom told her.

"So," the nurse said, looking back at me. "Now there are three of you."

"Three what?" I asked, confused.

"Diabetics." She paused. "No one told you there are two others here at school?"

My jaw dropped. *I wasn't the only one?*

"No," Mom said, squeezing my hand. "We weren't told."

"Sam, you can find their names on the lists up at the front of the classrooms. The lists let everyone know about the serious medical conditions some of our students have, like epilepsy or severe allergies."

"I've seen them," I said, nodding. "Diabetics are on there, too?"

"Absolutely," she said. "One of them is Evan Pinsky. I believe he's in your grade."

"I don't know him, but I know who he is," I told her.

"And there is a girl in grade eight who has type 2."

"Cool," I said. "I mean, it's not cool that they have diabetes, but—"

"It's nice to have something in common," Ms. Mitchell finished for me. "Even if it's something you don't want to have in the first place."

I was glad she understood.

While Mom and the nurse went over a bunch of

other details, I read the goofy nutrition posters on the wall and waited.

"Ready?" Mom asked when they'd finished talking.

"Definitely," I told her. I was more than ready to get back to my classroom and see everyone.

Mom gave me a big hug in the hallway. When she let go, she handed me the cell phone I was supposed to carry all the time. Kate had stuck a bunch of glittery butterfly stickers to it, so it would look more like an accessory than a life support. Mom had also put a sticker on it that said, *I am diabetic. Please dial 9-1-1*. It was in case I blacked out or had a seizure.

It was a smart idea, but kind of scary at the same time.

"You're going to text me every time you test your blood sugar, right?"

I nodded. "I will."

"And you won't hesitate to go see Ms. Mitchell if you don't feel well."

I nodded again.

Mom smiled. "I think we've got everything covered."

Between the cell phone, the plaid pouch that held my pen and insulin, my two medical ID bracelets and the blood-testing kit in my backpack, I felt like I was ready for outer space instead of a day at Evergreen.

"I look like a Transformer," I said.

"You look great," Mom said. "Call me if you need

to." She kissed my cheek. "For anything."

"I will."

"I mean it, Samantha."

"I know." I gave her a really big smile, so she'd know it was okay to leave me.

When she was gone, I took a deep breath and opened the door to Ms. Beane's classroom. English had already started.

"Samantha," she said, glancing at me over the top of her glasses. "We're glad to see you."

"Thank you," I said quietly.

I glanced around the room. Everyone was staring at me, but not like I was an alien or anything. They just seemed curious, like we'd all been when Drew Olsten broke his arm skateboarding and showed up in a cast.

I could handle that.

I walked down the aisle to my usual desk, which was next to Emily.

"Welcome back," she whispered.

"Thanks," I said, smiling.

Seeing her face made me feel the best I had all day.

We couldn't really talk in class, but during recess she walked with me to my locker.

"It's so cool that you're back," she said. "Good thing you'll be at practice tonight. I think Coach is going to name our captain soon."

I had to tell her the truth, but I hated to say the words out loud.

"Em?"

"Yeah?"

"I, uh, didn't say anything the other day, when you were at my house, but I'm kind of waiting to find out from my doctor if I can still play."

"You mean this Saturday?"

I cleared my throat. "I mean *ever*, Em."

"What?" she gasped. "What are you talking about?"

I told her about having to meet with Dr. Elliott before I'd know if I could play again.

"So, no one has actually told you that you won't be able to play."

"No . . . but it could happen."

"Sam," she sighed.

"What? I have to be prepared for the worst."

She shook her head. "I thought you were okay."

"I'm okay to come to school." I shrugged. "But soccer might be a different story."

"I don't even want to think about it. I can't imagine the team without you."

I couldn't imagine me without the team.

* * *

The day went well until math class. I was trying to test my blood before Mr. Edwards began the lesson, but someone noticed me. Suddenly, I felt like I was surrounded by TV reporters. Everybody had questions, beginning with what I was doing and moving on quickly from there.

"So," Brandon asked, "do you have to get shots?"

"Yup," I said, glad that my number was in range, and I didn't need one at the moment.

"All the time?" Sophia asked.

"Every day, but not all the time."

"Does it hurt?" Brandon asked.

"A little," I said, wishing we could talk about something else.

"What happens if you don't have a shot?"

I cleared my throat. "I get sick."

"Like puking?" Sophia asked.

"Kind of." I tucked my kit away and pulled out my textbook.

"What if—"

"I think Mr. Edwards is ready," I interrupted, pointing to the front of the classroom.

I did my best to focus on the lesson, but midway through class, I started to feel a bit low. I dug past the glucose tabs and pulled out a roll of Lifesavers. I unwrapped it as quietly as possible, then popped a lime candy into my mouth.

"Can I have one?" Madison asked, holding out a hand.

"Um, they're for emergencies."

She looked at me like I was crazy and dropped her hand back in her lap. "Whatever."

"Seriously, I just—"

"Samantha," Mr. Edwards interrupted. "I need your eyes up here, please."

"Sorry."

"Why does she get to have candy in class?" Madison demanded.

"Medical reasons," Mr. Edwards told her.

"Then maybe I need medical M&M's," Madison responded, and a few kids laughed.

"Let's get back to the lesson," the teacher said.

My face burned with embarrassment.

"Just ignore her," someone whispered from behind me.

I nodded, but I couldn't say anything.

Why couldn't I just be *normal*?

* * *

After the bell rang for lunch, Emily met me at my locker and watched me clean my hands with sanitizer. If my fingertip had anything on it, even something I couldn't see, I'd end up with the wrong blood sugar number.

The poke still made me flinch, but I was getting used to it. I squeezed a blood drop onto my strip and slipped it in the tester.

"Is it okay?" Emily asked.

"One hundred and ninety-seven", I told her when I got my reading. I looked around and saw some of the kids were pretending not to notice what I was doing, while others were totally staring. It was like math class all over again. "I'll see you in the cafeteria," I told her.

"You want me to go to the nurse's office with you?"

I shook my head and smiled. "I want you to save me a seat. I'll only be a few minutes."

I tucked my tester away and headed for Ms. Mitchell's office.

"So, how are things going so far?" she asked as she looked at my number.

"Fine," I told her. "A bit weird, you know. But fine."

"It might be a good idea to explain your diabetes schedule to some of your closest friends so they understand."

"I did," I told her. Emily was enough for now. The rest of the Strikers didn't need to know all the details.

"That's great, Samantha," Ms. Mitchell said. "Here we go." She pressed the button on my green pen, and we counted to ten as the insulin was injected.

By the time I got to the cafeteria, the place was packed. It took me a couple of minutes to get through the crowd to our table.

"Is everything okay?" Emily asked worriedly.

"It's fine," I said.

"You got a shot?"

"Yeah," I said. I unwrapped my sandwich.

"So, one ninety-seven. That's high, but not super-high, right?" she asked.

Emily's questions were starting to get to me. It felt good to have a friend who would watch out for me, but she didn't need to do it all the time.

I stared at the sandwich.

"And you'll have to test it again before you have an afternoon snack, right?"

I nodded again. It was one thing to watch out for me and another to be a diabetes stalker.

"Let it go," Mai muttered, looking uncomfortable.

"I just want to make sure she's okay," Emily said.

"I'm okay," I told her. "As long as you don't drive me crazy with questions." I smiled so she knew I was mostly joking.

"I'm just worried about you, Sam."

"I'm fine," I told her. "Really."

And for the rest of the day, I *was* fine. I wasn't asked a bunch of questions in class, although a few kids stared. I texted Mom every blood sugar reading. Except for feeling a bit sick to my stomach before afternoon recess, everything was pretty good.

Maybe, after a couple of days, I really would feel normal again.

* * *

By the next night, I was doubting that theory.

Zoe was mad because she wanted to cuddle with Mom on the couch, but I was already in her place. I was wrapped in a blanket, holding googly-eyed Clyde and feeling crummy, the way I sometimes did after my shot. I'd had a long day at school and was worried it would be a long night.

The last thing I wanted to do was move.

"Sit with Dad, Zoe," Mom told her.

"He's too bony. I want squish."

"I'll try to take 'squish' as a compliment," Mom said, laughing. "Honey, Samantha doesn't feel well right now."

"Me, neither," she said, hands on her hips. "I think I have diabetes, too."

"No, you don't," Mom said, giving her a look.

"How do you know?" Kate asked from her spot on the recliner. "No one knew Samantha had it until Saturday."

"*Do* I have it?" Zoe asked, panicked.

"No," Mom said firmly.

"What's for dinner?" Aiden asked. I was glad he'd changed the subject.

"Chicken and vegetables," Mom said. "Just like it says on the menu."

She'd decided to feed the whole family a healthier diet, so the whiteboard menu was for all of us. It was based on what the dietitian at the hospital had told us about carb counting. Our bodies turn carbohydrates into sugar, so for Mom to plan my diet, she needed to know how many carbs were in each serving of food.

"Seriously?" Aiden groaned, staring at the menu. "What about dessert?"

"We're not having dessert."

His eyes bulged. "What?"

"You heard me," Mom said.

"Why no dessert?"

"Because we're having baked potatoes."

"So?"

"So, baked potatoes are high in carbs. We'll have a little dessert tomorrow night, as the dinner I have planned is lower in carbs." She sighed. "I really wish you'd read up on this."

"I don't want to read. I just want to eat cake or ice cream, like we used to."

"This is healthier."

"For Samantha, you mean," he muttered.

"For all of us," Dad corrected.

Aiden groaned. "Why do we all have to be punished because *she* has diabetes?"

I couldn't believe it!

"Aiden," Dad warned.

"What?"

"Why am *I* being punished by having diabetes at all?" I snapped. "So you can't have a piece of cake or pie tonight. Big deal. While you're complaining, I'm the one feeling like I'm going to puke."

Mom's body stiffened. "Do you need to get to the bathroom, Samantha?"

"No," I sighed. That was the thing. I never actually threw up; I just felt like I might.

"I'm tired of this," Aiden said, getting up from the couch and storming out of the room.

"Well, so am I!" I shouted after him.

Chapter
ELEVEN

Once I got into the swing of dealing with the diabetes, I actually had a few days where I felt pretty good.

But that wasn't every day. Even when I did everything I should, like eating the right foods, taking shots at the right times and getting lots of sleep, I still had bad days. Some days I woke up feeling tired, thirsty and a little sick to my stomach, like that awful day on the soccer field, because my sugar was too high. Other times, I felt shaky, dizzy and sweaty because it was too low.

One morning I tested at two hundred and nineteen, so I went to Ms. Mitchell's office. When I got there, Bella Masterson was already waiting.

I'd never talked to her before, since she was a grade ahead of me.

"You're Samantha, aren't you?" she asked, totally taking me by surprise.

"Uh, yeah," I said, smiling. I sat down next to her.

"What's wrong with you?" she asked.

"Nothing," I answered, feeling kind of offended. "Why?"

"Uh . . . you're in the nurse's office?"

"Oh!" I said, blushing. "I have diabetes and—"

"Me, too."

I stared at her. Bella Masterson was the diabetic in grade eight? I never would have guessed. She seemed so *normal*.

"Are you here for a shot?"

She shook her head. "I'm type 2, so I don't get shots. Just pokes. I wanted to talk to Ms. Mitchell about something."

Type 2. Instead of needing medicine to keep her blood sugar in range, she could use plain old *food*. "You're lucky."

She stared at me. "What?"

"You're lucky," I repeated, then thought about it for a second. Lucky probably wasn't the right word. "I mean, you just have to watch what you eat and test your blood, right?"

No insulin shots, no gross glucose tabs and no Big Red.

Bella frowned. "I hate it when people say that."

Oops.

"Sorry, I didn't mean anything bad. I just—"

"Diabetes is diabetes," she interrupted. "None of it is *lucky*. And, anyway, some type 2 diabetics need medicine, too."

"Yeah, but . . ." I didn't know what else to say. "I'm sorry, Bella."

We sat in silence for a couple of minutes, which was totally awkward. Finally, I cleared my throat and said, "I hate diabetes."

She glanced at me but didn't say anything, so I tried again.

"I hate having to think about every single thing I put in my mouth."

"Same here," she said, smiling slightly. "My doctor put me on a special diet, and it's *so* boring. My mom cooks the special stuff for me, but keeps feeding the rest of my family regular food."

"Really?" That wasn't fair.

"Yeah, so I have to watch them eat all the good stuff."

"That stinks," I told her, glad that Mom's menu was the same for everyone. I thought about how Aiden had complained about the meals at our house. Mom was trying to make things easier for me, but she was also keeping my whole family healthy at the same time.

"You know what's crazy?" Bella asked.

"What?"

"I say that my mom's feeding them the good stuff, but that's not really true. They're getting the *good-tasting* stuff. Cake, potatoes, bread. But it's all loaded with carbs."

"That's what I have to keep track of." I sighed, picturing a chocolate-frosted cupcake.

"All those things taste good, but all that sugar . . . my family doesn't exactly need it." She sighed. "They're all overweight. Mom says 'pleasantly plump,' but you know what?"

"What?"

"My little brother, Nathan, isn't just 'plump' or 'chubby,' he's fat. And it isn't cute. It's . . . dangerous. You don't have to be overweight to get type 2, but if it already runs in your family, like it does in mine, you're much more likely to. I don't want Nathan to get it." She was quiet again.

"We think my dad's great-uncle had type 1," I told her. "My doctor says it's more random, like it can skip whole generations."

She glanced at me. "You just found out you have it, huh?"

I nodded. "I had to go to the hospital on Saturday, because I was so high. They started giving me insulin."

She bit her lip and said, "You know, I might need insulin shots someday, too."

"Really?"

"If I don't control my diabetes, by eating the right foods and everything, it could get worse." She cringed. "And even if I do everything right, I might end up needing insulin anyway. And no matter what I said before, about all diabetes being the same, I really don't want to get needles every day."

Neither did I.

* * *

At lunchtime, Emily was waiting for me at my locker.

"Did you see the nurse?" she asked.

I unlocked the door and piled my books inside. "Yeah. Bella Masterson was there."

Emily frowned. "Why?"

"She's type 2."

She looked confused. "What?"

"It's this other kind of diabetes," I said, pulling out my lunch bag and closing the door. "She's doesn't have to get needles, but she still has to test her sugar levels and all that."

"Oh," Emily said, walking toward the cafeteria with me. "So you talked to her about it?"

"Yeah. She was really nice. It felt good to talk to someone who's dealing with some of the same things I am."

"That's cool," Emily said, but it didn't really sound like she meant it.

"Bella is—"

"Hey," she interrupted. "Unless we want to ask for an extension, we need to finish our Ancient Egypt project."

"We don't need an extension." I didn't want to do the presentation after everyone else. "We can probably finish it at lunch tomorrow, and we'll bake our blondie pyramid the night before it's due. Okay?"

"Okay." She nodded. "You know, we could make it out of Lego or something like that."

"I think we should stick with the blondies," I told her.

"Are you sure?" she asked, looking concerned.

"Definitely."

"Cool. Hey, I was also wondering if you want to sleep over on Halloween."

"I'll have to ask my mom, but yeah, that would be fun."

Emily smiled. "We can watch scary movies after we trick-or-treat, and . . . oh." She winced. "We don't have to trick-or-treat. We could—"

"It's okay. I can still do it. I just can't eat the candy all at once, you know?"

"Sure," she said.

"I'll ask my mom tonight, but I'm almost a hundred percent sure she'll say yes."

I was a hundred percent wrong.

"I'm afraid not," Mom said when I brought it up.

"What?" I asked, stunned. She loved Emily, and I'd slept over at her place about a thousand times before. "Why not?"

Mom held the plates she was unloading from the dishwasher and stared at me like she was waiting for me to figure something out.

"Who's going to test you at midnight and four in the morning?" she finally asked.

"I can set an alarm and—"

"Who's going to give you a shot if you need one?"

"Oh," I said softly.

Mom tucked some hair behind my ear. "I'm really sorry, honey. This is one of those times where it would be a big help if you could give yourself shots."

"I don't want to," I told her. The idea scared me too much.

"Dr. Vincent said lots of kids do it. It's about being independent, Sam."

"What if I punctured one of my organs or something?"

Mom smiled. "It's not that big a needle. And you could always inject your arm or leg instead."

How weird was my life that I could only go to a

sleepover if I stuck needles in myself? "It's not fair," I muttered.

"Life isn't fair," Mom said quietly.

It was the kind of thing parents said because they knew there was no comeback.

"*Mom.*"

"We all have different burdens, and we deal with them. Adversity makes us stronger."

I groaned. "I don't even know what adversity is."

"Things not going your way. Obstacles in your path. Right now your obstacle is the diabetes and those shots."

"I told you already, Mom. I don't want to do it."

"Then I'm afraid a sleepover is out of the question, unless you have it here."

"But the whole point was to go to Emily's."

Mom shrugged. "I don't know what to tell you."

"Never mind." I sighed and started to walk away.

"You know, you've never been the kind of girl who gives up, Samantha."

"I'm not giving up."

"You could have fooled me." She went back to unloading the dishwasher.

* * *

Later that afternoon, I was trying to do homework in my room while my sisters played Scrabble.

It was a pretty unfair match, considering Kate was

a spelling-bee fanatic and Zoe was too little to spell much more than her name.

"That's twenty-six points for me," Kate said.

I glanced over my shoulder to see her happily scribble down the number.

"*Twenty-six?*" I asked, surprised. "What word was that?"

"Shh," Kate said. "We're trying to play."

"Yeah," Zoe echoed. "Shh."

I leaned back in my chair to read the word, which was JXQ.

"Kate!"

She whipped around to face me. "What?"

"That's not even a word!"

She scowled at me. "Mind your own business, Sam."

"You're cheating."

"You are?" Zoe asked, her eyes wide.

Kate crossed her arms. "Nobody said they had to be English words."

I raised one eyebrow at her. "So what language is *that?*"

"Don't you have some homework to do?" Kate snapped.

Seeing how serious she was, I couldn't help laughing as I rocked back in my chair. "You little weasel!"

The chair tipped further, and before I could get my balance, I fell over and landed right in the middle of the Scrabble board.

"Eek!" Zoe screamed as the pieces scattered.

"You did that on purpose!" Kate shouted.

I laughed until the bedroom door flew open.

"What happened? Is everyone okay?" Mom was out of breath.

"We're fine," I told her. "I just fell."

"How?" she demanded.

Kate and Zoe turned their heads back and forth between us like they were watching a tennis match.

"I lost my balance," I told her. "I'm fine, Mom."

She pressed one hand against her heart. "I'd appreciate it if you were more careful, Samantha."

"We were just joking around," I explained. "It was an accident."

"With your condition—"

"Mom, this had nothing to do with the diabetes. I just lost my balance, okay?"

She gave me a long look then sighed. "I don't need any more stress, Sam."

Before I could say anything, she had left the room and closed the door behind her.

What was *she* stressed about?

"Are you going to move?" Kate asked, standing over me with her hands on her hips.

I hadn't realized I was still on the floor, but it was surprisingly comfortable, and I didn't feel like going anywhere. I stared up at the ceiling and said, "I don't think so."

"But we're trying to—"

Before she could finish, Zoe crawled over and curled up next to me. "Can I be this close?" she asked, sounding worried.

I looked at her. "Definitely. You can be as close as you want."

"I won't hurt you?"

I shook my head, and when my hair rubbed against the carpet, it stood up on end with static electricity.

Zoe rubbed hers as well. Seconds later, Kate was lying on my other side, her hair as crazy as ours. We giggled for a minute, then fell quiet.

It didn't take me long to figure out what Mom had meant about stress. Sure, I was the one living with diabetes, but *she* was the one taking care of a diabetic. *She* woke up in the middle of the night to test me. *She* cooked food that would keep me healthy. And every time I stayed home from school, *she* missed work.

I felt Zoe's pudgy little fingertip trace a slow circle on my arm. I wasn't sure if it was the careful gentleness of her touch or thinking about my mom, but before I could stop it, a tear rolled down my cheek.

Chapter

TWELVE

The next day I had an appointment at the diabetes center. I was going to meet my diabetes "team," including Dr. Elliott, the endocrinologist. (Try saying that five times fast.) Their job was to help me stay healthy and on track.

Since Mom had missed so much work, Dad drove me to the office for my first appointment. Traffic was bad, so we weren't as early as he wanted to be. I walked in by myself while he found a parking spot.

There was no one in the waiting room, except for a little girl with short brown hair, cut in a bob.

"Hi," I said.

"Hi." She smiled.

"Are you waiting for somebody?" I asked, sitting in one of the empty chairs.

She looked at me like I was crazy. "Yeah. Dr. Elliott."

I stared at her. "*You* have diabetes?" She was so little!

She laughed. "Duh! That's why I'm here."

"How old are you?"

"Eight."

Only a year older than Kate! "And you're here by yourself?"

She shook her head. "My mom went to get jelly beans for when I'm low."

I had Lifesavers; she had jelly beans.

"Gotcha," I said, but she wasn't finished.

"I get to pick between jelly beans and Gummi Bears. Gummi Bears are best because I can bite their heads off, but the store in here doesn't have them."

"Oh," I said.

"The Safeway by my house has them. Seven-Eleven has them. Save-on-Foods has them—"

"But the store in here doesn't," I interrupted. "I got it."

She frowned at me and stopped talking.

After a few minutes, I got tired of the silence and was curious. "Do you have type 1 or type 2?"

"Type 1," she muttered.

"Me, too."

She looked me up and down. "How long have you had it?"

"I just got diagnosed."

Her eyes got wide. "No way!"

"How long have *you* had it?"

"Since I was a baby."

I'd never thought about a baby having diabetes!

"Not being able to eat what I want drives me crazy," I told her.

"I can eat what I want," she said. "Just not all the time."

"It stinks."

"Not really," she said, shrugging. "My little brother's allergic to peanuts, so he's never even tasted a Snickers or a Reese's Peanut Butter Cup. *That* stinks."

A dark-haired nurse came around the corner. "Oh!" she said with a big smile. She had bright pink lipstick on her teeth. "Two dia-beauties waiting! How are you doing, Rosie?"

"Good," the little girl chirped.

"And what's your name, hon?" the nurse asked me.

"Samantha Stevens."

She sat at the computer and ran a bright pink fingernail down the screen. "A-ha! A three o'clock appointment with the team. It'll just be a few minutes, okay?"

"Sure," I said.

She keyed something in, then disappeared again.

"I hate the shots," I told Rosie as I leaned back in my chair.

"You'll get better at it," she said matter-of-factly.

"What?" I asked.

"Giving yourself shots."

"Wait, you do your own?"

"Duh."

"But you're *eight*."

"I started when I was six, but only in my arms and legs. I didn't start doing my tummy shots until this year."

I stared at her, totally shocked. "Are you kidding?"

"No. Three of my dia-buddies slept over last Saturday, and we *all* did our own shots."

"Dia-buddies?"

Rosie grinned, showing off the spaces left by three missing teeth. "Kids I met at diabetes camp."

"Diabetes *camp*?"

That sounded like the worst place on earth!

She shrugged. "Uh-huh. I go every year."

"What do you do at diabetes camp?"

"Same stuff as regular camp. Play games, ride horses, make crafts and all that. The only difference is that all of the campers have diabetes. Oh, and there are nurses there. They help with the pokes and shots."

I was stunned into silence. An all-diabetic camp?

The more I thought about it, the cooler it sounded. It would be nice to hang out with a bunch of kids who weren't scared and didn't have a bunch of questions.

The campers would already know exactly what it was like to have diabetes.

"I'm getting a pump," Rosie said, out of nowhere. "Pretty soon."

I remembered Dr. Vincent trying to talk to me about pumps back at the hospital. I'd been so overwhelmed, I hadn't been ready to listen. "What is it?"

"It's like a little box you wear on a belt. It feeds you insulin through a tube that's attached to your body. That way you don't have to get shots all the time. My friend loves hers."

"And you're—"

"Did you go on the walk last week?" she interrupted.

"What walk?"

"*Hello*? The walk for JD."

"What?"

"Juvenile diabetes." She paused. "We are juveniles with diabetes, right?"

"I guess so."

"Anyway, I collected over six hundred dollars this year."

"What for?"

She rolled her eyes. "It's a *fundraiser*."

"A fundraiser," I repeated.

"Yeah, we're raising money to help find a cure."

"A cure would be nice," I told her, nodding.

"Seriously. It'll be cool to get the pump, but I don't want one for the rest of my life. I want to be *cured*."

* * *

When Dad and I met Dr. Elliott, she introduced us to Colleen, who was a dietitian, and a nurse named Sean. They asked a thousand questions about how I was feeling and how things were going.

Dr. Elliott wanted to know who was tracking my carbohydrates and testing my blood.

I glanced at Dad, then back at the doctor. "I test my blood sugar, but my mom figures out what I can eat. My dad helps, too. They do the shots."

"What about at school?" Sean asked.

"I go to the nurse's office."

Dr. Elliott sat back in her chair and gave me a long look. "I think it would be best if you started handling more of this on your own."

"What?" Dad and I both gasped at once.

Dr. Elliott smiled. "This is pretty simple math we're talking about. It's just a matter of learning how to do it."

"But—"

"This is will give you more independence, Samantha. The more you're able to do yourself, the more you'll feel like a normal kid."

"But I'm not normal," I said quietly.

She shook her head. "Learning how to handle this

disease is the best thing you can do."

I looked at Dad, who said, "I think that makes sense."

I thought about Rosie, who was giving herself stomach shots and talking about her diabetes like it was no big deal.

I wanted to be like that.

"Um, okay," I said. "I can try."

"That's the spirit," Dr. Elliott said.

We tackled the math first. I had to use my blood test number to figure out how many carbs I was allowed. That wasn't too bad. I'd been overwhelmed at the idea of figuring out how many carbs were in every bit of food I ate, but to my surprise, Dr. Elliott and Colleen made it easy. Colleen even had a little booklet, some charts and a cheat sheet of everyday foods.

After some practice, I knew I could handle the calculations myself. And that *would* make me more independent.

But I was hoping for even better news.

"Uh, Dr. Elliott?" I asked as we were leaving the office.

"Yes?"

"Can I . . . I mean . . ." I took a deep breath before blurting, "Can I go back to playing soccer?"

It only took her a couple of seconds to answer, but it felt like days.

"Sorry, Samantha," she said, shaking her head. "You and your body are making some big adjustments right now."

"Oh," I said, taking a shaky breath.

"We're still figuring things out, and we want your sugar levels to be more stable."

"But—"

"And we've got to focus on your education as a diabetic, too. You have survival skills to learn, like how to recognize the symptoms of high and low sugars."

I nodded. "I understand."

"That isn't a *no* to soccer, Sam. It's a *we'll see*."

"Okay." I was disappointed, but at least there was still hope.

* * *

That night I asked to use the computer and did a bunch of reading about insulin pumps. I wasn't a doctor, but it seemed like I would be a good candidate. And if I was using a pump, I would be way more independent.

"Mom and Dad," I said, handing them the pages I'd printed out, "I really think this would be a cool thing to have. It would help me and make my diabetes easier to deal with for everyone."

"What is it?" Mom asked, leaning in to read along with Dad.

"An insulin pump. I was talking to a girl at Dr.

Elliott's who's waiting to get one. I wouldn't have to mess around with shots anymore."

They both kept reading and flipped to the next page.

I waited until they were finished to ask, "Well?"

"I think we'd have to do a bit more research," Dad said.

"And talk to Dr. Elliott," Mom added.

"Definitely," I agreed. "Wouldn't it be awesome, though?"

Mom smiled. "It does seem like a pretty amazing tool, Sam."

"So we can check into it?" I asked, getting excited.

Mom and Dad looked at each other and smiled.

"Sure," Dad said. "Let's see about getting you one."

"Yes!" I practically screamed.

* * *

Suddenly, I was feeling good about everything. The more I thought about the pump, the more excited I got.

I'd been doing so well, I decided to celebrate with a treat. I figured if I saved my sugars for after school, I could enjoy fresh-baked pyramid blondies with Emily.

I felt a bit nauseous after English, so I went to the bathroom and got out the glucose tabs. But when I thought about how gross they tasted, I threw them out. I could tough it out for one afternoon, I was sure. Mind over matter.

Walking home after school, I started to feel a little sick again. But the blondies would be ready in an hour, and I was already picturing them drowning in a big scoop of melting vanilla ice cream. Ooh! I could add chocolate sauce, too. A blondie sundae was worth waiting for, even if I felt gross in the meantime.

"So," Emily said as we dropped our backpacks by the kitchen table. "I found this recipe online for diabetic blondies and—"

I shook my head. "Let's just make regular ones." It had been forever since I'd had a treat, and I wanted a *real* one.

"But you're—"

"The only diabetic in the class. No one else should have to suffer because of it."

"Suffer?" she snorted. "Sam, eating a diabetic blondie isn't going to hurt anyone."

"And eating a regular one isn't going to hurt *me*. I can't wait to have some of these things, so let's get baking."

She stared at me. "Wait. You're going to eat 'some?'"

"Yeah. I didn't have any sugar today."

She frowned. "I thought you were supposed to balance your blood sugar throughout the day so—"

I was starting to get annoyed. Probably more annoyed than I would have been if I'd eaten properly, but

I didn't want to think about that. "Are you a doctor, Em?"

She cleared her throat. "No. But you aren't, either."

"It's fine. I have everything under control."

"But I'm worried that—"

"Em! Just let it go, okay?"

"Hi, girls," Mom said, coming into the kitchen from upstairs. "I didn't hear you come in."

"Hi, Ms. Stevens," Emily said.

Mom hugged me, then my best friend. "It's so nice to see you. What are you guys up to?"

"Building our pyramid," I told her. "Our presentation is tomorrow."

"Sounds good," she said. "I'm just zipping out to the bank. The girls are upstairs, and Aiden should be home any minute." She gave me a quick once-over. "You're good?"

"Totally good," I told her.

Emily and I got to work, tripling the recipe I'd found in one of Mom's cookbooks and adding the ingredients into a big bowl. We were quiet at first; I think we both felt bad about arguing. But then we started to chat again.

I told Emily I couldn't sleep over on Halloween. She seemed disappointed, so I tried to cheer her up by telling her about the pump and how it could help me be more normal. Talking about it was also a good distraction from the slight dizziness I was feeling.

"So this pump is stuck to your body all the time?" she asked, looking up from the recipe.

"Yeah, it's a little computer that automatically delivers insulin when I need it. Rosie told me she's getting one and—"

"Who's *Rosie*?" she asked.

"This girl I met at my doctor's appointment. She's getting a pump because one of her dia-buddies has one and loves it."

"Her dia-buddies?"

"Sorry," I said, smiling. "That's what they call the friends you make at diabetes camp."

Emily frowned. "There's a camp?"

"Yeah, all the campers there have diabetes."

She nodded slowly. "Maybe you and Bella should go."

"What?"

"Your new best friend, Bella Masterson."

"What? She's not my—"

"Or even better, the three of you could go together. You, Bella *and* Rosie."

"What are you talking about?"

"Those are the people you have stuff in common with, right?"

"We all have diabetes, yeah, but—"

"And I don't," she said, her voice tight.

I was totally confused. "You wouldn't want it, Em. I hate it and—"

"Never mind," she said, looking at the book again.

"What's going on?" I asked.

"Nothing, okay?" She kept staring at the page.

"Not okay," I told her. "What is it?"

She sighed. "It's *this* . . . dia-buddies and special camps and pumps and . . ."

I stared at her. "I have diabetes, Em."

She shook her head, sadly. "This is the worst thing that's ever happened to me."

"To *you*?"

"Yeah, I—"

"Was sick on the soccer field?" I snapped.

"No, I—"

"Get woken up twice every night for a shot?"

"No, I—"

"Can't eat what you want, whenever you want? Get tired for no reason at all?"

"I know you have all this stuff going on! And if it's such a big deal, why did you skip all your sugars today? For blondies? That's a stupid thing to do, Sam."

"I've *earned* one stinking treat! You don't know what this is like."

159

"Sam!" she said, getting frustrated.

"What?" I snapped again, tired of everything. The conversation *and* the dizziness that was starting to get worse.

"When I said it's the worst thing that's ever happened to me, I meant—"

"Hello? It didn't happen to *you* at all. *I'm* the one who got diagnosed, and *I'm* the one who has to deal with all of the junk that comes along with it."

She glared at me. "You're not even listening to me."

"Because you aren't making sense! How the heck is diabetes the worst thing that's ever happened to *you?*"

"*Sam.* The worst thing that's ever happened to me is—"

"What?" I'd never been so mad at her.

"Losing my best friend," she said quietly. Then she picked up her backpack and left the kitchen.

"Then go find another one!" I shouted after her. "That's what I'm going to do!"

I heard the door close behind her, but didn't move.

Whatever. I'd build the stupid pyramid myself.

I grabbed the cookbook, and I was trying to focus on the slightly blurry words when I heard the door open again.

I found myself hoping it was Emily, but Aiden walked into the kitchen instead.

"What's Emily's problem?" he asked. "She didn't even say hi to me in the driveway."

"She had to go home," I muttered, squinting at the page.

Aiden poured himself a glass of milk, then headed into the living room. I heard the thunder of two sets of feet running down the stairs, accompanied by lots of giggling.

It was only a couple of seconds before the girls were arguing with Aiden over the remote.

The page got even blurrier and my knees started to shake, but I was determined to wait for those blondies. Like I told Emily, I'd *earned* them.

I reached for the baking tin, and the next thing I knew, I'd landed on the floor with a crash.

When I opened my eyes, my blurry brother was standing over me shouting, "What's wrong?"

It felt like it took every bit of strength I had to whisper, "Low sugar."

"Get the tabs!" Kate shouted at Zoe.

I couldn't keep my eyes open, but I heard my little sister unzipping every pocket on my backpack.

"I can't find them!" Zoe cried.

"Look harder!" Kate yelled, opening one cupboard after another and slamming them closed.

All I could see was the silver packet of tabs dropping into the garbage can at school.

"Where's Mom?" Aiden shouted, but I had no energy left to answer him.

"What about juice?" Zoe shouted. "Can't we give her juice?"

"Yes!" I wanted to shout.

But then everything went black.

Chapter
THIRTEEN

When I woke up, I was still on the floor. It took me a couple of seconds to realize that someone was stroking my hair.

And that someone was Mom.

My whole body flooded with relief.

"She's awake," Zoe whispered, and I looked over to see her tear-stained face.

Mom leaned over, and I saw her face was filled with worry. "You're back," she said, starting to smile. There were tears in her eyes, too.

"That's good," a man's voice said, and I saw two paramedics standing behind her.

"You called an ambulance?" I asked.

"Aiden did," Mom explained.

I heard footsteps and turned my head to see my brother disappear through the doorway.

"How do you feel?" the female paramedic asked.

"Weird," I told her. "A little queasy, I guess."

I heard a sniffle and saw Kate in the corner. As soon as our eyes met, she burst into tears.

"Why is everybody crying?" I asked, confused. "What happened?"

Mom cleared her throat. "Why don't you tell me what happened first?"

I licked my lips. "What do you mean?"

"*Samantha.*"

"I just . . . I don't know, I—"

"Kate used Big Red," Zoe announced.

"What?" I gasped.

"You were jerking around and—" Kate began, but Mom cut her off.

"You had a *seizure*, Samantha."

My stomach felt hollow. "I did?"

"You fell, and Zoe couldn't find your tabs," Kate said.

"We tried to give you juice, but you wouldn't wake up," Zoe added, her bottom lip quivering.

"And you," I asked, looking at poor little Kate, "you got Big Red."

Kate nodded. "I was scared, but I remembered the video."

"She saved your life," Mom whispered. "And now I want to know why your seven-year-old sister had to do that."

I took a deep breath and told Mom what I'd done. Saving my sugars for blondies. Throwing away my tabs. Trying to be normal.

And failing.

She shook her head and made "tsk" noises the whole time I was talking.

When I was finished, the female paramedic asked, "Are we ready?"

"Yes," Mom said, then told my sisters that Aiden would be in charge until Dad got home. "And that's only about half an hour from now." Then she looked at me. "Let's go, Sam."

"Where?" I asked.

"To the hospital," Mom said firmly.

"But I'm okay now."

"How do you know that, Samantha?" she demanded. "You just had a *seizure*."

I didn't really have an answer for that.

* * *

I ended up spending the night in the hospital, which was awful, especially when Dr. Vincent heard about what had happened. He didn't hold back when he told me how disappointed he was in my behavior.

Mom brought Kate and Zoe in to visit the next morning. They were still worried about me. The nurses gave them both shiny stickers and gushed over them for saving my life.

"*Zoe* didn't do anything," Kate grumbled at one point, but a stern look from Mom nipped that attitude in the bud.

"Thank you," I told them once the nurses had left. "You guys really did save me."

I'd broken down in tears a couple of times, thinking about how scared they must have been and what I'd put them through. I pulled both of them into a tight hug.

"Ouch!" Kate finally said, pulling away.

I didn't ask about Aiden, and none of them mentioned his name.

* * *

It wasn't until I came home that I realized I'd missed our pyramid presentation.

Of course, Emily had been right to worry. It was a stupid idea to save my sugars for the blondies.

But I still wasn't sure what she meant about losing her best friend.

No matter how many times I turned that over in my head, it never made sense. I hadn't *gone* anywhere. And the fact that she was jealous, because I'd met some other kids with diabetes, wasn't fair at all. Talking to people who were dealing with some of the same things that I was, had really helped me. Was I supposed to feel *guilty* about that?

I thought about calling her, but I couldn't do it. I missed her and wanted to make up, but I felt like it was her job to apologize first.

When I arrived at my locker on Monday morning, she wasn't there waiting for me. I had a big lump in my throat, but I pretended everything was fine as I got my books together.

Emily didn't say a word to me in English class.

Things only got worse at lunchtime. I joined the Strikers at our usual table, but Emily wasn't there.

"Hey, Sam," Mai said, sliding over way more than she needed to make room for me.

"So my mom's going to drop me off at six-thirty," Sara said to Kylie. "Is that cool?"

"Definitely," Kylie said, nodding. "Mai and Brianne will be there a little later, but we can get started on the cupcakes while we're waiting."

"What are you guys talking about?" I asked.

Kylie turned to look at me, surprised. "Oh, just this thing at my house."

"Thing?" I asked, waiting for more.

She glanced at Sara, then Mai. "Yeah, just a little get-together."

"For the Strikers?" I asked, wondering why I hadn't heard about it.

"Uh-huh," she said, nodding slowly.

"So, when is it?" I asked, excited about hanging out with my teammates again. It felt like it had been forever.

Mai started to answer, but Kylie cut her off. "Aren't you . . . *sick*?"

"No."

"I didn't invite Alyssa either, since she has the flu."

What? I hadn't told anyone about my trip to the hospital, though I had missed a day of school. Was it the diabetes?

"I'm not contagious." I glanced at Mai and Sara, hoping for support, but they just looked uncomfortable.

"Well," Kylie said. "You're kind of not on the team right now, either."

I felt like she'd punched me in the stomach. "I'm still on the team," I told her. "I'm just not playing right now."

"That's what I mean." Kylie shrugged. "You're not playing."

Tears started to prick my eyelids, but I was determined not to let them fall. I didn't know what to say, so I shoved my half-eaten salad into my lunch bag and stood up.

Mai said, "You don't have to leave, Sam."

But I did.

I almost called Mom to pick me up, but decided not to. Even though she'd said I could call her for anything, I knew she had missed a lot of work because of me already, and I didn't want her to get in trouble.

The person I really wanted to see was Emily, but I had no idea where she was.

I walked back to my locker. The hallway was busy, but even though I was surrounded by kids, I'd never felt so alone.

* * *

When the bell finally rang to end the day, I couldn't get out of school fast enough. All I wanted to do was get back to my room and climb into bed. I wanted blankets over my head, and Tony cuddled next to me.

My fight with Emily was bad enough, but Kylie's comment about me not being on the team really hurt.

What if she was right?

What if Dr. Elliott told me I couldn't play soccer anymore?

If diabetes took that from me, too, I didn't know what I'd do.

Because of the way my day had gone, with every step I took on the way home, I felt more certain that Dr. Elliott was going to break my heart at my next appointment.

When I opened the front door, I started toward the stairs, but I heard Dad's voice coming from the kitchen. He sounded angry.

"What's going on?" I asked Mom. She was sitting at the kitchen table while Dad paced the room, talking on the phone.

"Your pump," Mom said.

"I'm getting one?" I gasped. For a split second, I forgot about everything that had gone wrong. A pump could change everything for me!

"He's—"

"Ordering a pump?"

Mom shook her head. "Just trying to get some answers, honey."

She told me Dad had been on the phone, transferred from one person to another, for almost an hour.

"Why?"

"We can't get one right away." She paused. "We have to wait."

"They don't have any left right now?" I asked. "They're waiting for a new shipment?"

"No. We have to wait until you're more stable and have been for a while."

"Are you kidding?" I practically choked.

She shook her head.

Suddenly Dad slammed the phone down. "I just

spoke to the supervisor's manager's director and got nowhere."

"How long do I have to wait?" I asked.

Dad shook his head slowly. "A year."

"That's ridiculous . . ." Mom began, then took a deep breath. "A pump will be good for her, Jason."

"I know," he said, rubbing his forehead. "But that's the policy. Unless we pay for it ourselves, we have to wait for a year."

"There we go!" Mom said, smiling.

"Cool!" I said, starting to smile.

"Beth," Dad said. His head shook very slightly. "We need to talk about this." He glanced at me, then back at her. "In private."

"What?" I asked. "It's about *me*. Shouldn't I be part of this conversation?"

He was quiet for a moment or two, and when he spoke, his voice was very soft. "It would cost thousands of dollars . . . or we can wait a year and get one for free." He looked both sad and embarrassed. "I'm sorry, Sam."

"It's okay," I told him through the lump in my throat.

We didn't have the money.

* * *

I'd been lying on my bed for about half an hour when Mom knocked on my door.

"Come in," I said.

"Nice to have the room to yourself for a change?" she asked, sitting on the edge of the bed.

"Yeah. Where are they?"

"Playing next door. How are you doing?"

I sighed and started to get up. "Hold on, my tester's in my backpack."

"No," Mom said, pulling me back onto the bed. "Not your blood. How are *you* doing?"

"Oh." I flopped onto my pillow. "Crummy."

"Why's that?"

I told her about the fight with Emily and Kylie's party. "I wasn't even invited."

"It's hard for them to understand what's happening, Samantha. They'll come around." She gave me a long look. "What else is bothering you?"

"Giving up soccer," I said, and I couldn't hold back the tears anymore.

"Whoa," she said, pulling me up and into a hug. "Why? Don't you want to play anymore?"

"I do!"

"Then what's the problem?"

"Doctor Elliott's going to tell me I *can't* at my appointment tomorrow."

"Says who?"

"I just know she will."

"Samantha," Mom said, letting go of me so she could

look into my eyes. "We don't know what she's going to say."

"But—"

"We've been told that part of dealing with diabetes is getting exercise."

"I know, but—"

"And soccer is exercise. I don't see why you'd have to give it up." She shook her head. "There's no use worrying about it now, honey. You'll have an answer tomorrow."

* * *

After dinner and a couple of rounds of Go Fish with Kate and Zoe, I joined Dad on the couch to watch some TV. I wasn't really paying attention, though. I was still worrying about what Dr. Elliott would say about soccer.

I wished more than anything that I would still be allowed to play with the Strikers.

If wishes were nickels, we'd all be rich . . .

A few weeks ago all I wished for was the thrill of being named team captain. But everything had changed so much . . . and so fast. I didn't want diabetes to ruin my dreams, but maybe it already had.

"Dad, when you and Mom say I can still do anything I want to, even though I have diabetes . . . are you just saying that to make me feel better?"

He shook his head. "Absolutely not."

"But—"

"I say it because it's the truth, Samantha."

I wanted to believe him, but I wasn't sure I could.

"It doesn't feel that way," I told him. "Everything feels different now. Harder."

"That's why it's important to be positive."

"You and Mom keep saying that, but it's tough."

"Life isn't always easy, Samantha."

"I know *that*. I just want things to be . . ."

"What?" he asked, waiting for me to go on.

Normal.

"Never mind," I told him. "It's nothing."

He got off the couch and held his hand out to me.

"What are you doing?" I asked, taking it.

"What are *we* doing," he corrected.

"Okay, what are *we* doing?" I asked as he pulled me toward the hallway.

I trailed him into the office and sat down on the little white stool he pulled over to the desk. He settled into the big chair in front of the computer.

"Name a dream."

"What?" I asked, confused.

"Name a dream of yours. Anything you've ever dreamed about doing or being."

"Seriously?"

He laughed. "Yes, seriously. Come on, Triple S. One measly dream."

"Okay. To be a professional soccer player." *Obviously.*

"Perfect," Dad said, and he started to type.

"What are you doing?" I asked.

"Looking up professional athletes with type 1 diabetes."

I stared at him, thinking it was a joke, but he was too busy typing to notice.

"You really think there are some?" I asked doubtfully.

"I'm sure of it," he said, just as a website popped up. "A-ha! Right off the bat, we've got two female professional golfers and an NHL player." He turned to smile at me. "How easy was that?"

I scooted closer to the screen so I could read the list of athletes. It was way longer than I'd expected. I saw a bunch of football players, basketball stars, an Olympic gold medalist in swimming and even an Ironman triathlete.

I couldn't believe it.

All of those people, all of those *professional athletes*, had diabetes?

I started to smile.

"I don't see any women's soccer players here," Dad said. "You know what that means, don't you?"

I shook my head. "No."

"It means you can be the first."

I grinned. "Come on, Dad."

"I'm serious, Sam. Someone has to be first. Why not you?" He smiled. "*Why not Triple S?*"

He started typing again, and another screen popped up.

"Look, here's a list of other famous people who have type 1. Actors, artists, politicians . . . Just look at them all."

And I did.

In fact, Dad and I kept searching online for another half-hour or so. With each minute that passed, I felt a little bit better. The people we read about were doing all kinds of awesome and amazing things. Obviously diabetes wasn't giving them superpowers or anything, but it wasn't stopping them either.

It made me feel . . . hopeful.

Chapter
FOURTEEN

The next day I was so determined to stay positive about my appointment that I decided not to worry about parties I wasn't invited to, insulin pumps that I'd have to wait for or even fights with (former?) best friends.

Mom picked me up after the last bell. My heart pounded the whole way to the diabetes center.

"Relax, Sam," Mom said as she pulled into a parking space.

"I am," I told her.

"You could have fooled me," she said with a smile. "Now, let's go hear some good news."

I took a deep breath and opened the car door, hoping against hope that I was minutes away from the good news I'd been dreaming about.

This time, it was just the doctor and Sean, the nurse.

"Well," Dr. Elliott said, "I heard about the seizure."

My face got hot.

"Lesson learned?" Sean asked gently.

I nodded, thinking of my seven-year-old sister having to use Big Red. "Yes."

"So, how have you been feeling since the incident?" Dr. Elliott asked.

I glanced at Mom, who nodded for me to go ahead. "Pretty good. Today, I mean. Not all the time."

"That sounds about right," the doctor said. "It's a tough adjustment, isn't it?"

I nodded. It took all of my self-control to not ask about soccer. Instead, I answered questions about carbs, blood tests, insulin shots, sleep, moods and about a hundred other things. I hoped all my answers added up to me doing well enough to play again.

Dr. Elliott wrote notes as I talked, and sometimes she asked for more information from Mom if she needed it.

"I think things are going well, overall," she finally said, leaning back in her chair. "I know there are bumps in the road. Some of those bumps can be avoided," she added, looking at me, "and some of them can't. Type 1 can be pretty overwhelming."

I nodded again.

"It sounds like you're getting a handle on the disease,

though," she said, looking from me to Mom.

"We're getting there," Mom said, giving my shoulders a squeeze.

"So, do either of you have any questions for me and Sean?" Dr. Elliott asked.

Before I could blurt my big question, Mom asked her about test strips and a bunch of other things that *weren't* soccer. I tried to be patient.

"What about you, Samantha?" Dr. Elliott asked when they were finished talking. "Any questions?"

"Um," I said. I licked my lips, which were suddenly dry. "I wanted to ask about . . . soccer. I mean, whether I can still play soccer."

She smiled, "Yes, you can."

"What?" I almost screamed. I leapt out of my seat and jumped up and down.

"Hold on a second," she said, directing me back to my chair. "Exercise is a very important part of living with diabetes, but there are some rules that go along with that."

"Anything!" I said, reaching for Mom's hand and squeezing it.

"You can't overdo it right away."

"I won't!"

"I mean it. You've got to ease back into things. Soon enough, you'll be able to play the way you always did, but you'll have to make some adjustments. Your body is going to react differently to exercise than it used to. You'll have to monitor your blood sugar before, during and after the game to make sure you don't go too low, or even too high. You have to pay attention to how your body's responding to the activity." She turned to Mom. "I recommend that you talk to the coach, the other parents and her teammates about the diabetes. It's important that they recognize the signs that her levels are low."

"I can do that," Mom said, squeezing my hand back.

"I have some pamphlets," Sean said. "You can hand them out to the parents. It couldn't hurt to give some to Sam's teachers as well."

Dr. Elliott looked at me. "You've made it pretty clear how much soccer means to you, but you have to promise me two things."

"What?" I asked, suddenly worried.

"If you start to feel that something isn't right while you're out on the field, you have to promise me that you'll let your coach know that you need to take a break and figure out what your body is telling you."

I weighed the options of standing on the sidelines or collapsing on the field and knew I'd have no problem keeping *that* promise. "Sure! What's the second one?"

"I want you to promise that you'll have fun out there."

"Of course I will!"

I was so happy, I hugged her and Sean.

* * *

That night, the Stevens family raised a toast to me and my return to soccer. I tried to ignore the fact that Aiden barely lifted his glass. He hadn't even commented when he'd heard my great news.

Kate and Zoe more than made up for his lack of enthusiasm, though. They ran upstairs after we ate, but not before they told all of us to stay exactly where we were.

"I'm going to my room," Aiden announced as soon as they were out of earshot.

"Not a chance," Dad said. "You can clear the table, though."

It only took a couple of minutes for the girls to come back down, giggling all the way. When they came through the door, they were wearing feather boas and shiny dresses that were much too long for either of them.

"Ready for our cheer?" Kate asked.

"You're supposed to be cheerleaders?" I said, before I could stop myself.

"Not supposed to be," Kate said. "We *are*."

"We *are*," Zoe echoed.

"Well, we're ready," Dad said with a smile. "Let's hear it."

There was a lot of whispering and elbowing as they got lined up.

"Tonight, if possible," Aiden grumbled.

"Shh," Mom said, shooting him a dirty look.

"Ready?" Kate finally asked.

"Yes, we're still ready," Dad told her.

"Okay, here we go. One . . . two . . . three."

They took two steps forward, one back, then waved their hands and started to chant, "Samantha, Samantha, she's our man—"

"She's your what?" Aiden snorted.

"If she can't do it," they continued, "no one can!"

"Do what?" Aiden muttered.

"S!" Kate shouted, throwing her hands up and wiggling her fingers in the air.

"A!" screamed Zoe, doing the same.

"M!" Kate bellowed.

And then there was silence.

"Uh . . ." Zoe bit her lip.

"A," Dad whispered.

"What?" Zoe whispered back.

"A," we all said.

"A!" she shouted.

Silence again, until Kate muttered, "I lost my place."

"Sam is good enough," I told them.

"That was wonderful," Mom said, clapping her hands. "Good job, girls!"

"Can I go to my room now?" Aiden asked.

"Why don't you hang out with us for a little while?" Mom suggested.

"I just did," he told her. He refused to even look at me. "So, can I be excused?"

Mom glanced at me, like I had to be okay with it.

And I wasn't.

But I also wasn't going to let my mopey brother ruin one of the best nights I'd had in forever.

I shrugged, and half a second later, Aiden disappeared.

Kate and Zoe were chattering Dad's ears off, but over the noise, I heard Mom murmur, "I'm going to call him back down here."

As much as I wanted my brother to be a part of things, I didn't want him there by force.

"You can't *make* him hang out, Mom."

She raised one eyebrow at me. "Sure, I can."

"Yeah, but I don't want you to," I said quietly.

She frowned. "What's wrong, Sam?"

I felt the sting of tears and shook my head so they wouldn't fall.

It didn't work.

Mom pulled me into a hug, which was really awkward since both of us were sitting down. "What's going on?"

"Aiden hates me."

She gave me a squeeze. "No, he doesn't."

"Ever since I got sick, he's been acting so mean, like it's my fault. He's a total jerk," I said, sniffing. "And don't tell me it's because he's a teenager."

"I think you should talk to him."

"He'll just tell me to get lost."

Mom let go of my shoulders and held my face in her hands. "Go talk to him, Samantha."

"It won't do any—"

"Right now," she said.

I sat for a couple of minutes, listening to my sisters giggle and shriek. Then I took a deep breath before I got up and started toward the stairs.

As I climbed, I wondered what I was going to say to him. I had no idea why he was so mad at me. Missing out on a few desserts wasn't much of a reason. Feeling inconvenienced by my disease wasn't either.

Aiden was supposed to be my big brother, my protector. But he was acting like my enemy instead. He, and Emily, seemed to be taking *my* disease personally.

There was no answer when I knocked on his door,

but the music inside was really loud, so I knocked again, even harder.

He yanked the door open. "What?"

I cleared my throat. "Can I talk to you?"

He didn't move to let me in. "You're talking to me right now."

He wasn't going to make this easy. "Can I come in?"

Aiden opened the door wider but didn't say anything. That seemed to be the closest thing to an invitation I was going to get, so I stepped into the room and sat on the edge of his bed. "What's going on?"

"Huh?"

"Can you turn down the music?" I shouted.

He scowled and turned it off completely.

"So . . . what's going on?" I tried again.

He barely looked at me. "What do you think?"

"I think you're being a creep," I snapped, my hurt feelings quickly turning into anger. "Why are you being so mean to me?"

He glared at me. "I'm not—"

"Yes, you are, Aiden. Ever since I found out I have—"

He cut me off. "*Diabetes.*"

"Yes," I snapped. "And I'm mad at you! You didn't even care when I thought I'd have to give up soccer." I paused. "Then again, you didn't care about giving it up yourself, so—"

"What?"

"You're the best soccer player I know, and you dropped it like it was nothing!" I glared at him. "Ever since I was diagnosed, all I could think about was how important soccer was to me and how much I wished I could be out there on the field. I would have given anything."

"Sam," he said, but I wasn't finished.

"You could have been out there doing what I loved, but you hung around here, in this stupid, gloomy room, instead." I couldn't control my disgust. "What a waste."

"Sam," he said again.

"Then, I find out I *can* play, and you're such a total jerk that you can't even be happy for me. You just—"

"Look, I'm *mad* you're diabetic, okay?"

"Join the club! And, by the way, it's not *my* fault!"

"No, you don't get it." He sighed. "I'm not mad at *you*."

I waited, but he didn't explain. "Then who?"

He shook his head. "I don't know. Mad at the diabetes. Mad that things have been so weird around here since you went to the hospital."

"Weird, how?"

"Mom and Dad are worried all the time, having to constantly check on you and . . ."

"What?"

"They don't have time for stuff anymore."

"Like what?"

"Taking care of the girls. I've been letting Zoe sit with me in front of the TV and testing Kate on her spelling words."

I didn't point out that he should have been doing that all along. That was part of being a big brother.

"Mom was testing Kate this morning," I reminded him.

"You know what I mean."

"No, I don't. Things are different around here for me, Mom and Dad. The rest of you guys can still do whatever you want."

He stared at me. "Are you kidding me? Our kitchen is in, like, lockdown mode. I can't even make a snack."

"You couldn't really make a snack before," I joked.

He smiled, but only for a second. "Well, the cupboards are full of medicine now and—"

"Not all of them. And what are we supposed to do with it?" I asked. "Leave it on the floor?"

"You're missing my point."

"The point? What, that you're mad I have a disease that's wasting cupboard space and forcing you to be nice to your little sisters?"

"No!" he practically shouted. "Don't you get it?"

"Get *what*?" I shouted back, ticked off that he was being so selfish.

He groaned and rubbed his face before looking at me again. When he spoke, his voice was shaking.

"I'm mad . . ."

"Yeah, I got that part."

"Let me finish. Sure, I'm mad because everything's changed, but mostly I'm mad because I have to worry about you."

"Worry about—"

"Yeah," he said, cutting me off. "I worry about you *all the time*. I worry that something's going to go wrong, and no one will know how to take care of you. I worry that you're going to collapse on the field, at school, in the backyard, or just about anywhere, and no one is going to know what's wrong or what to do."

I held up my wrist, my medical ID bracelet shining. "That's why I wear this thing."

"But what if people don't see it? Or they see it, but they don't know what it means?"

"It says right on the back that I have—"

"What if you black out again? Now that you're going back to soccer, it could happen. Or what if you black out at home again and Mom and Dad aren't here?"

"It was okay, Aiden."

"Because Kate, *our little sister*, saved you."

"Well, yeah. But you called 9-1-1."

"Too little, too late." He shook his head. "Knowing

that gigantic needle is waiting in the kitchen for the next time it happens—"

"It's easy to use, Aiden. You just—"

"Stab you with it?"

I winced. "Not *stab*. Inject."

He closed his eyes. "If Kate hadn't been there—"

"You would have done it," I said firmly.

He sighed. "It *totally* freaks me out that your life would be in my hands."

I was shocked to see that there were tears in his eyes.

We were both quiet for a few seconds.

I thought about how things used to be between me and Aiden, before he started high school and had to act cool. I thought about how he'd been the person I went to when I had a nightmare or needed help.

He'd always saved me.

"My life's been in your hands before," I reminded him.

He sniffed and wiped his nose with the back of his hand. "What are you talking about?"

"You're my big brother," I said quietly. "You've always protected me."

"No, I haven't."

"You pulled me out of the waves that time at the beach."

"You thought you could swim to Australia," he said,

shaking his head and kind of laughing. "Dork."

"You made sure I didn't get trampled by all the big kids when I started school."

"You were, like, the smallest kid in the whole school. They would have crushed you."

"You taught me how to double-knot my shoelaces."

"What, so I saved you from tripping to death?"

"I'm just saying." I shrugged.

He was quiet, and then he said, "I can't believe I just *froze* when you had the seizure. I'm so sorry."

"It's okay, Aiden."

"It's not, though. It's really serious, like life and death. It's complicated and messed up and—"

"No, it isn't," I told him. "It's really simple, Aiden. I trust you."

"But geez," he said, running his hand through his hair. "Big Red?"

"I trust you," I repeated. "Just like I always have."

* * *

I felt so good about how things had gone with Aiden, I knew I had to make up with Emily. Suddenly, it didn't matter who apologized first. I missed her too much, *and* I couldn't wait to tell her my awesome soccer news.

When I got to school, I dumped my bag in my locker and started searching the hallways for her. I found her standing in front of the vending machine in the cafeteria.

"It's a little early for KitKats, isn't it?" I asked.

Emily spun around, obviously surprised to see me. "Oh . . . hi."

"Hi," I said, but before I could say anything else, she started to walk away. I grabbed her arm. "Em."

She tensed. "What?"

"I'm sorry."

"For what?" she asked, looking doubtful.

"That I yelled at you," I told her. "That I missed our presentation."

She shrugged. "Ms. Handel was totally fine with the extension." She was quiet for a moment. "Where were you?"

"In the hospital."

"What?" she gasped.

"I had a seizure after you left my house."

Her face paled. "I didn't know, Sam. I would have—"

"You tried, Em. You knew I was being stupid about the blondies and my blood sugar. You were right about everything."

"I'm sorry, Sam," she said quietly. "And I'm sorry I got angry at you, too. I think I was just jealous."

"Of the diabetes?" I asked.

"No," she thought about it for a second. "It's just that

when you told me about it, I thought it would be this thing that we fought together, you know?"

I nodded. "Sure."

"So, I tried to be a good friend and support you, but you didn't want to talk about it." She took a deep breath. "But then it seemed like you *did* want to talk about it, just not with me. It seemed like you only wanted support from Bella and Rosie."

"Please don't be jealous about me having diabetic friends, Em."

"Sometimes I can't help it." She paused. "I feel left out when you talk about things like camp and hanging out with Bella in the nurse's office and—"

I shook my head. "You're my best friend in the whole world. You don't have to be jealous of anybody. Seriously, it's only been a few days since we stopped talking, but do you have any idea how much I missed you?"

She smiled. "I missed you, too."

We were both quiet for a moment, and I figured it was as good a time as any to try to explain how I was feeling.

"You know, I can't figure out which is worse, having diabetes, or figuring out how to deal with it."

"What do you mean?"

"I'm different now, right?" I waited for her to nod. "And I want people to understand how things have changed for me."

"I know. You need to test your blood and get needles and stuff."

"Right, but I don't want people to feel sorry for me because of it. I don't want them to treat me like I'm sick all the time."

And suddenly I realized why. "Because that makes me feel like I *am* sick all the time. And I'm not. I have mornings when I wake up feeling awesome. I have afternoons when I feel perfectly normal." I smiled. "Sometimes I'm scared, and sometimes I feel like all I want to do is puke, but when I'm feeling good, I want to enjoy it. I don't want people acting worried all the time."

"I can't help it, Sam. I get worried and—"

"Of course you do. You're my best friend. But it's not your job to worry, just like it's not my mom's or my dad's or even Aiden's. All I need is for people to *understand*. Sometimes I'll need help, and I'll tell you when I do."

"Really?" she asked.

I nodded. "Really."

She looked relieved. "I'm just so glad you're here, Sam. I mean, nothing's been the same without you. School, soccer—"

"Oh! Oh! Oh! *That's* what I wanted to tell you! My doctor gave me the okay to play soccer!"

"She did?" Emily asked, sounding as excited as I was.

"Yup. I'm back on the field for Saturday's game."

"That's perfect! Oh my, gosh, I'm so happy, Sam!"

I was glad she felt that way. "So, are we good?" I asked.

"Yeah," Emily said, grinning at me. "We're good."

Chapter

FIFTEEN

I woke up Saturday morning with that old, familiar feeling of excitement. *Game day!*

I didn't hear the usual snoring from my sisters' bunk bed, which meant they were already downstairs. I showered and dressed in my uniform. Then I checked the weather outside and added track pants and a jacket.

I was super-excited to play against the Cougars. They were a tough team, but we'd beaten them before, and I was pretty sure we could do it again.

When I walked into the hallway, I saw that Aiden was halfway down the stairs.

"You're up?" I gasped.

"Duh. You've got a game today, don't you?" he asked, smiling. "I can't miss that."

I grinned at the back of his head, happy that he was coming.

Mom had made waffles, and my stomach growled at the sight of them. I wished I could have one, but I checked the whiteboard and headed for the pantry to get some cereal instead.

"Sam, these are for you," Mom said.

"The waffles?" I asked, surprised.

"I found a website with all kinds of recipes. These are made with whole grains and—"

I was too excited to let her to ruin my waffle moment.

"Let's just pretend they're regular old original recipe waffles, okay?" I said, reaching for a plate. "They smell awesome."

I sat between Zoe and Kate, who were gobbling their waffles like eating was a timed event. Like they didn't mind the whole grains a bit.

* * *

We gave Emily a ride, and when we got to the field, Coach Donaldson came over to talk to Mom. I knew I was the topic of discussion because Coach was whispering.

Mom nodded a couple of times, and then Coach blew her whistle and called out, "Can I get all of the Strikers and Striker parents to huddle up over here?"

As they all gathered around with curious looks on their faces, I started to feel nervous.

Coach told the group that Mom had an announcement to make, and Mom cleared her throat. I guess she was nervous, too.

"I think most of you know that Samantha had an incident on the field a few weeks ago." She looked from one face to the next. "What some of you may not know is that she was diagnosed with type 1 diabetes."

"Oh, no," one of the mothers gasped.

Mom smiled and continued. "Our family has learned a lot about the disease, and we've learned how determined Samantha is to be out on the field as part of this team. I have some information here about her condition, and I'd appreciate it if you would take the time to read it with your daughters and understand what we're dealing with."

Mom pulled the rubber band off Sean's pamphlets and started handing them out.

"Most importantly," she said, as she handed one to Kylie, "I want you to understand that Samantha is the same twelve-year-old girl she was before this diagnosis. She can still do almost everything she used to . . . when she has the opportunity."

When Mom was finished, the Strikers hit the field to warm up. As I rounded a cone, dribbling the ball, I looked up to see a few of the parents hovered around Mom, asking questions.

And that made me feel really good.

So when Kylie avoided me as I dribbled toward her, I was more than ready to speak up for myself.

"Uh, it's not contagious," I called out to her.

"What?" she asked, stopping.

"My diabetes," I explained. "It's not contagious." She glared at me and started to turn away. "But I guess being a jerk is."

"Excuse me?" Kylie snapped.

The other Strikers had stopped what they were doing to listen.

Sara walked over to us. "What's that supposed to mean?"

I took a deep breath. "Ever since I got diagnosed, some of the people on this team have been acting like jerks."

Having an audience made me nervous, but I pushed ahead anyway. "They've left me out of things and made me feel bad." I took another breath and glanced at Emily, who nodded. "Being a jerk doesn't *have to be* contagious."

Kylie actually blushed. "I don't know what you're talking about."

There were a lot of things I could have said at that moment. A lot of mean things. But what was the point?

We were supposed to be a team, working together.

"If you really don't know how you made me feel, you need to listen to what I'm saying. I have diabetes, and it isn't contagious. You don't have to be scared to be around me. It doesn't stop me from playing soccer or hanging out with friends. It doesn't stop me from having my feelings hurt, either."

Kylie and Sara looked at each other and rolled their eyes. But Mai was looking embarrassed.

She walked toward me. "I'm sorry, Sam," she said quietly.

"Thanks, Mai."

"This is stupid," Kylie said. "I'm done with this conversation." She and Sara dribbled away from us.

I watched them go, disappointed by the way they'd acted but ready to move on.

"You okay?" Emily asked.

I nodded. "Who wants to warm up?" I said, tapping the ball in front of me and starting to jog.

In a matter of seconds, the rest of the Strikers were right behind me.

When we got into the passing drills, the ball zipped past me to the sidelines, stopping in front of Aiden. He froze for a second, then started dribbling. He flicked the ball upward with his foot, then bounced it off one knee, then the other.

"Show-off," I said, teasing him. The truth was, it was cool to see him playing with it.

"I'm open," Mai called to him.

My brother bumped the ball high with his right knee, then headed it over to her.

"Now *that* was awesome," Mai said, and I could tell the rest of my teammates were impressed, too.

Aiden shrugged, like it was nothing, but I knew he loved it.

* * *

When the game started, there wasn't much of a crowd on the sidelines, but my sisters made up for that. They were jumping around and cheering like a couple of maniacs.

It was surprisingly easy for me to shove Kylie's and Sara's attitudes to the back of my mind.

It felt so perfect to be back out on the field, I couldn't stop smiling. The girls were the same, the rules were the same and, most importantly, the happiness I'd always felt when I played was the same.

And that was a huge relief.

But then, partway into the first half, my knees started to get shaky.

I thought about what Dr. Elliott had said about not overdoing it, but I wanted to stay in the game. My team needed me to score.

I told myself it was probably just nerves or something.

"I'm open," I shouted, and Emily passed me the ball.

I started dribbling toward the far goal, ready to make a big play.

"Go, Samantha!" I heard Mom shout.

I kept running, my heart pounding in my chest. When I got close, I looked for a clear shot, but there wasn't one. I kept dribbling, blowing past the defense like it was nothing.

But it wasn't nothing.

I felt like throwing up, but I kept going. I wasn't going to let diabetes ruin this. But instead of feeling the rush of adrenaline I usually did when I kicked into high gear, I felt dizzy.

I finally passed the ball and bent over, trying not to draw any attention to myself. But I knew Mom would be watching me like a hawk. I looked at my hands, fingers spread out on my knees, and all I saw was blurriness.

Kate's face flashed in my mind, along with images of Big Red and the emergency room.

I sighed and lifted an arm so Coach could see I needed to take a break.

In other words, I gave up.

"It's okay," Mom said when I met her on the

sidelines. "You haven't been out there in a while, Sam." She watched me test and when she saw the result, she handed me a glucose tab.

Gross.

"Thanks." I sighed.

"You'll have to work your way back to the shape you were in before. And remember what the doctor said? Lots of running will have an effect on you."

I hated feeling so weak.

I felt like I'd let everyone down. And even worse? I knew that Coach Donaldson would never pick a part-time player for team captain.

My sugar was fine early in the second half, so Coach put me back in. My mind was focused on one thing: scoring.

I dribbled toward center, but got blocked by a defender and passed the ball to Emily. She dribbled closer to the goal, but there were two players on her right away.

"I'm open!" I shouted, and she passed the ball back to me.

It was my big chance. My moment to shine!

I eyed the goalie, who was crouched and ready for me. I moved left, then right, trying to find the perfect spot for my shot.

"Go for it, Triple S!" I heard Aiden yell from the sidelines.

I tapped the ball with the toe of my cleat, took a deep breath and gave it everything I had.

The ball soared through the air, but so did the goalie, who caught it at the last second.

I didn't waste time feeling bad about it.

"Let's keep the pressure on," I called out to my teammates, staying positive. "We can do this!"

But it turned out that "we" didn't include me.

Coach Donaldson pulled me out midway through the half to give me a breather. To be honest, I was glad she did, because I was feeling pretty tired.

At the same time, I wished she'd left me in because Emily was playing her best game ever. While I stood on the sidelines, she scored twice in just a few minutes.

"Great shot!" Coach called out to her after the second one. "Wow, she's been a dynamo lately," she said, turning to me.

I nodded, missing the days when I was the dynamo.

Suddenly, I saw that Emily would be the perfect choice for team captain. She'd been at every practice and every game. She was a good player and she was only getting better. I hoped like crazy that Coach would choose her over Kylie.

From the sidelines, I focused on being happy for Emily and imagining how excited she would be when

Coach told her the great news.

* * *

We won the game by a single goal, which was scored by my best friend. Perfect! When we all got into a huddle to shout "Two, four, six, eight," she wore the biggest grin I'd ever seen on her face.

After, I started to walk toward my family, but Coach Donaldson asked me to help carry her cooler back to her car.

Once we'd put it in the trunk, Coach closed the hatchback. When she turned around, she had something in her hand.

"This is for you, Samantha."

She held out a bright white C.

My jaw fell open.

She was making me team captain?

Me?

My heart pounded in my chest. My dream had come true!

I took the letter and held it in my hand, staring at it.

"I wanted you to accept it before I made the announcement to the team," she explained.

I thought about how badly I'd wanted it and how sure I'd been that I'd lost my chance. Kylie was leading the team in goals. Emily never missed a practice, and she was always doing her best on the field.

So, why was Coach Donaldson giving the C to me?

Then I realized that I knew the answer.

I felt my cheeks burn.

She felt sorry for me.

Stupid diabetes was ruining everything!

I took a deep breath, and even though it physically hurt to do it, I handed the C back to her.

"I can't take it," I told her, hoping I wouldn't make everything even worse by crying.

Coach Donaldson frowned. "I thought you wanted this, Samantha. In fact, I was *sure* you wanted this."

"I did," I told her. "I mean, I *do*, but not like this."

"Like what?"

"You know," I said, and then I waited for her to nod. But she didn't, so I had to say it. "The diabetes."

She tilted her head and stared at me like she'd never seen me before. "You think I'm offering this out of pity?"

"Well . . . yeah."

She shook her head. "Samantha, team captain is a reward, but it's also a responsibility. When I gave you this letter I wasn't feeling sorry for you; I was *challenging* you."

"Challenging?"

"I'm going to expect more from my captain than I do from anyone else on the team."

"But—"

"I need someone I can rely on to energize the rest of the girls, to show good sportsmanship and to do their best. I need someone to be a leader."

"But I might not be able to play as much as I did before."

She shook her head again. "Everyone has their turn on the sidelines."

"But when I get low, I miss shots, and—"

"*Samantha.* No one plays perfectly all the time. If they did, no one would miss a shot and no one would miss a save. How could that work?"

I thought about that for a second. It *couldn't* work. No one could ever win . . . or lose. "It wouldn't," I admitted.

"Exactly. Nobody is at their absolute best for every second of the game." Her voice got quiet and she looked into my eyes. "That's true off the field, too. We all have our best and worst moments. Sometimes the worst ones can be *really* tough. But we can't have the best ones without them."

I thought about that for a moment. I'd never been more devastated than when Mom was going to ban me from soccer for a week, or when I'd talked myself into thinking that Dr. Elliott wouldn't let me out on the field again. On the other hand, I'd never been happier or more excited than when Mom changed my punishment and when the doctor gave me the okay to play.

"I think I know what you mean," I told Coach.

"I don't need a captain who spends every second on the field and makes every shot that comes her way. I need someone who is strong," she tapped the side of her head, "up here."

"Me?" I asked quietly.

"Yes. You're a very strong girl, Samantha."

"Um . . . thank you."

"So, do I have my captain?" Coach asked.

I nodded as I started to smile.

And when I held that C in my hand, I was grinning.

Chapter
SIXTEEN

A few weeks after I became team captain, I wound up getting really sick. I caught a virus and couldn't keep any food down, which wasn't exactly great for my blood sugar levels. It was kind of depressing to know that it was exactly the kind of "bump in the road" that Dr. Elliott had warned us about. The kind we couldn't really do anything about. I had a disease, and sometimes that disease called the shots.

I didn't have to go to the hospital, but I missed almost a week of school *and* soccer. During lunch on my first day back at school, I joined the rest of the Strikers at our usual table.

"Hey, Sam," Emily said. She stopped peeling her orange and looked up at me.

"Hey," I said, slipping my sandwich out of its baggie.

"I hope you don't mind," she said, smiling kind of shyly at me, "but I told the team about that insulin pump."

"Oh." I took a bite of my sandwich, feeling a little self-conscious.

I hadn't forgotten about the pump, but I *had* started giving myself shots. I was getting pretty good at it, even though it freaked me out at first. Emily's mom was also learning how to do them, so I could sleep over at their house like I used to. It was pretty cool, but the pump would have been better.

"We know you have to wait a year," Emily said. "But—"

"We might have a way to come up with the money so you can get one sooner," Mai blurted.

I looked at the other girls, who were smiling.

I shook my head. "No, you guys. It's, like, *thousands* of dollars."

"Sure," Emily said, "but we're thinking Sportsville could help."

I stared at her. "The store?"

"Yeah. They sponsor hockey and basketball teams. They host skateboard competitions . . ."

"So?"

"So, we should ask them if they want to help you." Mai grinned.

"She's not a *team*," I heard Kylie mutter from the far end of the table.

"Or a charity," I added, embarrassed. I didn't want people to feel sorry for me.

"Of course, you aren't," Emily said, elbowing me. "But you're an *athlete*, right?"

"Yeah," I answered, doubtfully.

"And we're thinking they could sponsor an athlete."

"How?" I asked.

"They could chip in money for every goal you score this season," Brianne suggested. "You know, like a pledge."

I liked the sound of that. "I'd be earning the money instead of them just giving it to me." I started to smile. "That's a cool idea."

"Maybe we can do some team fundraising, too," Emily said.

I noticed Sara moving a little closer to the conversation . . . and away from Kylie. "What about a car wash?" she suggested.

"Or a bake sale?" Mai chimed in, and then it seemed like everyone started calling out ideas.

I couldn't help grinning, thinking of all the possibilities. I was super-excited that my teammates wanted to help. I glanced at Kylie. Well, most of them, anyway.

While Mai wrote a list, Emily leaned a little closer to me. "Like you said, maybe a pump could help you feel more . . . normal, you know?"

I agreed that the pump would be an awesome thing to have, and it would be a huge help to me and the rest of my family.

But it wouldn't make me normal.

And that was okay.

Because the truth was, I *wasn't normal*.

I was a type 1 diabetic.

But that wasn't all.

I was also the team captain for the Strikers (complete with a white C above my heart).

I was a sister, a daughter and a best friend.

I was strong, positive and surrounded by people who cared about me (even my teenaged brother).

I may not have been "normal," but that was okay.

Because I was actually pretty lucky.

Acknowledgments

Huge thanks to Diane Kerner for suggesting that I tackle this topic and for her guidance along the way. Also to Jennifer MacKinnon for her tireless efforts and eye for detail. Thank you for being so patient! Thanks to Aldo Fierro for designing the perfect cover. And, as always, thank you to Sally Harding, super-agent.

I'd also like to thank Rayzel Shulman, MD, FRCPC, of the Division of Endocrinology at the Hospital for Sick Children for her professional insight, and Nicole, Bonnie and Ella for sharing their personal experiences with type 1.